SEA &
COASTAL BIRDS

of North America

SEA &
COASTAL BIRDS

of North America

A Guide to Observation,
Understanding and Conservation

Scott Leslie

KEY PORTER BOOKS

Copyright © 2008 by Scott Leslie

Library and Archives Canada Cataloguing in Publication

Leslie, Scott, 1963-

Sea and coastal birds of North America : a guide to observing,

understanding and conservation / Scott Leslie.

ISBN 978-1-55470-045-5

1. Sea birds—North America—Identification. 2. Bird watching—North

America—Guidebooks. I. Title.

QL681.L45 2008   598.097   C2007-905702-0

ONTARIO ARTS COUNCIL
CONSEIL DES ARTS DE L'ONTARIO

THE CANADA COUNCIL | LE CONSEIL DES ARTS
FOR THE ARTS | DU CANADA
SINCE 1957 | DEPUIS 1957

The publisher gratefully acknowledges the support of the Canada Council for the Arts and the Ontario Arts Council for its publishing program. We acknowledge the support of the Government of Ontario through the Ontario Media Development Corporation's Ontario Book Initiative.

We acknowledge the financial support of the Government of Canada through the Book Publishing Industry Development Program (BPIDP) for our publishing activities.

Conservation status maps courtesy of NatureServe. 2006. NatureServe Explorer: An online encyclopedia of life [web application]. Version 6.1. NatureServe, Arlington, Virginia. Available at www.natureserve.org/explorer.

Key Porter Books Limited
Six Adelaide Street East, Tenth Floor
Toronto, Ontario
Canada M5C 1H6

www.keyporter.com

Design: Marijke Friesen
Electonic Formatting: Alison Carr
Printed and bound in China

08 09 10 11 12 6 5 4 3 2 1

NatureServe

For Connie, who loved the sea.

TABLE OF

CONTENTS

PREFACE

For many, the image of a "seagull" comes immediately to mind when seabirds are mentioned. Indeed, gulls are an important element of the coastal ecosystem. The diversity of bird species in the marine waters and along the coasts of North America extends far beyond gulls, however. There are a wide variety of seabirds, from the robin-sized storm-petrel to the enormous American white pelican with a wingspan of over 9 feet. Comical-looking puffins, magnificent gannets, piratical jaegers, nomadic shearwaters and noisy terns, and many others, lend the spice of life to the waters surrounding the continent.

If you were to stretch out every shore of every island, bay, inlet and cove of the coast of North America into a straight line, it would be hundreds of thousands of miles long. Along each of these miles, at some time of the year, you are bound to find birds. Whether it's a New Jersey beach covered with 10,000 migrating dunlins in May, a cliff on Devon Island in the high Arctic where the midnight sun slants into a colony of a hundred thousand nesting black guillemots, or in the crashing surf along the coast of British Columbia where a raft of harlequin ducks is tossed in a winter storm, there is hardly a spot along the continent's coasts that isn't host to its own unique assemblage of avian inhabitants.

Observing seabirds and coastal birds can be relatively easy when you visit accessible nesting colonies in the summer, the right shorebird beaches during migration or when you take a seabird boat cruise along one of our coasts. Yet, because these birds disperse widely at sea or along the coasts in winter, the non-breeding lives of many of them remain poorly known. Perhaps we will never know much more about them than we do now. This is not necessarily a bad thing, since it's good to still have some mysteries.

BIRDS AT THE EDGE OF A CONTINENT

On all these shores there are echoes of past and future; of the flow of time,
obliterating yet containing all that has gone before; of the sea's eternal rhythms—the tides, the beat of the surf,
the pressing rivers of the currents—shaping, changing, dominating;
of the stream of life, flowing as inexorably as any ocean current, from past to unknown future.
—Rachel Carson

The wind-driven fog swirled around me as I approached Cape St. Mary's on a typical July day on the island of Newfoundland. I could hear and smell my mist-bound destination well before I could see it. The rising, chortling din of gannets, the cries of kittiwakes and the muffled groans of murres were music to my ears. The pungent, yet not unpleasant, odor of tons of accumulated guano triggered a visceral memory of this seabird city in the North Atlantic.

Not until I reached the cliff could I see the eagle-sized gannets circling through the fog overhead. Hundreds of them wheeled above thousands more that were tending to their chicks atop a precipitous sea stack. Swarms of black-legged kittiwakes cried their namesake *kittiwake-kittiwake* call as they arrived at cliff-face nests with food for their chicks, while others set off to sea to look for more. Each followed a careful flight path to avoid colliding with the much larger and less maneuverable gannets. (They never *seem* to collide!)

Common and thick-billed murres came and went from the lower

Northern gannets nesting at the Cape St. Mary's seabird colony in Newfoundland and Labrador

cliffs, little black and white missiles on whirring wings. Several wily ravens patrolled the cliff-face in search of an unattended kittiwake or murre chick to eat, while North Atlantic waves broke 300 feet below me on the shore.

Every summer, seabirds are drawn from around the ocean to colonies like this one. When the urge to breed calls, they leave the relatively solitary life of an ocean traveller behind to become urbanites in a densely packed, bustling city of birds. In contrast to most land birds, which tend to disperse widely through their appropriate habitats during the breeding season, ocean birds tend to congregate at relatively few nesting sites. (Shorebirds generally work just the opposite way, breeding over wide areas while congregating at a relatively few, crucial feeding areas during migration. And sea ducks tend to be quite dispersed at all times of year though they will often form flocks in winter.)

Of course, breeding colonies are not located randomly, and such concentrated gatherings wouldn't exist if they didn't provide some benefit for the birds. First and foremost, nesting seabirds must be reasonably close to a reliable, easily accessible food supply so that they can feed their young frequently. For instance, the small fish known as sand lance have been historically abundant in the waters off puffin and kittiwake colonies in both the Atlantic and the Pacific, providing these birds with a dependable food source. Sites that are chosen for colonies must also have the right physical geography for nesting, such as appropriate cliff ledges for kittiwakes or thick sod for puffins to burrow in. In addition, they must have enough space for multiple nesting pairs, since, with the general exception of shorebirds, nearly all seabirds and coastal birds are colonial. Nesting sites must also be inaccessible to mammals that would wreak havoc on a colony as they prey on eggs and birds, hence the preference for islands or difficult-to-reach cliffs and headlands.

Because of the concentrated nature of such colonies, naturalists and scientists have been able to closely study many seabird and coastal bird species over the decades. This has made it possible to conduct population counts at individual colonies so that year by year comparisons can be made to determine the trend of seabird populations and the ecosystems that support them. Such long-term

A group of Atlantic puffins atop a cliff during the breeding season

studies have meant that the breeding biology of many species is well known, although much of their natural history in the non-breeding season—when they are at sea—is not well understood.

Unfortunately, the traits that have made these birds so well adapted to their ocean and coastal environments have also made them vulnerable to declines and possible extinction. Worldwide, of the 217 species of birds that have become extinct over the past 400 years, over 200 were on islands. Currently, nearly two-thirds of all threatened bird species live on islands.

Because of their strong loyalty to a particular breeding site, most seabirds are drawn like magnets, year after year, to specific nesting colonies and adapt only slowly to changes in the suitability of these locations. Even if breeding grounds are no longer suitable—for example, when important prey species in the waters surrounding them decline or collapse—the birds will often continue to return, despite negative consequences such as reduced success in rearing the young due to a lack of food. The islands, beaches and dune areas that are ideal nesting sites for seabirds and coastal birds are often also coveted by humans (especially along the eastern seaboard of the U.S. and the California coast where the human population, and the development pressure, are greatest). Approximately half of all wild coastlines and islands are likely to be developed as our numbers continue to grow. Because of this, many prime breeding, migratory and wintering habitats may be degraded or destroyed outright.

Birds that breed in large colonies on offshore islands in more northerly regions such as the North Atlantic and North Pacific may not be threatened by direct development, but they are susceptible to other human activities. One look at the tragic tale of the great auk will confirm this. At one time, the great auk was abundant throughout the North Atlantic. This giant, flightless seabird (the *only* flightless bird in the Northern Hemisphere) stood nearly 3 feet tall and lived exclusively on offshore islands. Hunting and egg collecting by fishermen and sailors wiped the species out by the mid-1800s. It was mercilessly exploited and is little more than a memory now. Puffins, murres and other auks were also exploited; fortunately they were more numerous to begin with and are still with us, but it wasn't for our lack of trying. Killing seabirds (or taking their eggs) was like shooting fish in a barrel, since the birds were, in essence, "captive" on their breeding site and could be quite easily preyed upon by humans. People who settled on offshore islands brought destructive animals with them, often not knowing the impact their pets or livestock would have on the island's ecosystem. Rats and other pests also arrived as stowaways on ships and fishing boats. These introduced species would often wreak more damage on seabird populations than deliberate exploitation by humans and they continue to do so today on many islands.

The defining characteristic of the true seabirds is their nomadic life at sea. They are as much creatures of the oceans as are whales and fish. Although largely species of the sky and the surface of the sea, seabirds have the ability to exploit prey living on or just beneath the surface.

Some birds, such as the auks, gannets and a few of the sea ducks, take this skill a step further. By using highly efficient diving techniques to extend their effective habitat well below the surface, they penetrate deeply into the sea (up to 600 feet in the case of the common murre) to capture prey. They are truly marine creatures.

During migration and in the winter, many marine birds will spread out across the Northern Hemisphere. (Some, such as the sooty shearwater, wander *both* hemispheres.) Ocean habitats are occupied in much the same way that terrestrial birds occupy different niches on land. At one extreme are the shearwaters, fulmars, albatrosses and petrels that wander far from land over the high seas. They are nomads of the vast oceanic

Black-legged kittiwakes beside the cliffs of their northern breeding grounds

wilderness, routinely covering tens of thousands of square miles during the non-breeding season in their search for ephemeral food supplies such as surface-schooling fish and squid. At the other end of the spectrum are gulls, terns and shorebirds that grace the coasts, rarely traveling more than a few miles from shore. That is not to say, however, that some of these coastal species don't cover enormous distances as well—the Arctic tern is the champion of long-distance migrants, journeying up to 25,000 miles in one year. For thousands of years these species have been evolving as they adapt to the changes that have taken place in both the marine and coastal environment.

In the past, seabirds and coastal birds have survived long-term fluctuations of ocean and air temperatures, ocean currents, sea levels and sea ice cover. Each of these changes can affect the availability of food and hence the energy birds need to expend to find it, the suitability of colony locations, the timing of the breeding season and overall reproductive success. But birds have been around for millions of years; they are resilient and adaptive and such natural vicissitudes have been enfolded into their genes through thousands of generations of evolution through natural selection. In the past, however, these environmental changes generally occurred slowly enough (usually over thousands of years or longer) to allow birds to adapt and extinctions were a rare occurrence.

The challenge now facing all marine species, whether birds, fish, mammals or even invertebrates, is the speed at which changes appear to be occurring in the ocean. The timescale for global change that was once on the order of millennia or longer has been replaced by one of much shorter duration, on the scale of decades. In other words, global warming promises to accomplish in just a few generations what used to take nature thousands of years to produce. On top of climate change, we are removing fish from the oceans at an unprecedented rate—fish that are an integral part of many of the same ecosystems that birds rely on. We also add enormous amounts of pollutants to the oceans. There is certainly no shortage of challenges facing seabirds and coastal birds. And we shouldn't take too much comfort in the fact that they have survived the countless volleys that have been fired at them by nature over the eons, because this time it's different.

Back on Cape St. Mary's, the sun had burned off the fog, revealing an infinite blue sea and sky speckled by whitecaps and white clouds; spectacular cliffs topped by a verdant green coastal heath that seems to go on for miles and miles; and, of course, the birds. Some 70,000 of them on the cliffs, in the swells and in the air. A swarm of 5,000 gannets wheeled above the colony, a spattering of brilliant specks on a canvas of blue. Pink moss campion, golden heather and other Arctic-alpine plants grew in profusion among the trailing juniper and black crowberry that covered the headlands behind the birds. Nobody really knows how long the colony at Cape St. Mary's, or any other seabird colony, has been around. But, standing in such a place and watching in awe this thriving city of birds at the edge of a continent, it was easy to imagine that it had always been here, and that it always will be.

Typical North Atlantic seabird nesting habitat

FACING THE CHALLENGES:
HOW SEABIRDS DEAL WITH THE UNIQUE DIFFICULTIES OF LIFE ON THE OCEAN

The oceans cover over 70 percent of the Earth and account for more than 90 percent of the total biosphere (the actual space inhabited by life on the planet). Millions of square miles of surface area and hundreds of thousands of miles of coastline, not to mention the immense *volume* of the oceans, would suggest an illimitable habitat for seabirds, coastal birds and all manner of other marine organisms. Indeed, the extent of marine and coastal habitat is huge, obviously encompassing an area greater than all the land on Earth. Parts of the ocean are like deserts with very low biodiversity, while other places, such as coral reefs, rival the species richness of a tropical rainforest. Areas of the ocean with low biodiversity may in fact have a high biomass, a situation that exists in many cold northern waters where there are very large populations of relatively few species.

And, just like on the land, different habitats in the ocean environment are occupied by different species. Habitats for terrestrial birds can vary considerably from one plot of land to the next. For instance, an aspen grove located beside a bog might be home to a group of bird species that is distinct from another group right next to it. Within such habitats there are numerous niches created by the topography, vegetation, forest openings and so on. The sea doesn't offer as wide a variety of niches (except on coral reefs), and though it is certainly much more than a vast homogenous wilderness, its lower habitat variety has resulted in fewer species of birds.

Northern gannets performing their spectacular dives in the pursuit of fish

In fact, since birds first evolved as terrestrial animals and only later adapted to life at sea, it is not surprising that their diversity is lower compared to land birds. There has simply been less time for species to evolve in the marine environment. Fewer niches to fill and less time to do it— that's why only between 3 to 4 percent of the approximately 9,000 bird species on Earth are seabirds.

Generally, seabirds and coastal birds live in a harsh environment where there is little opportunity to escape the elements. They must withstand extreme cold at high latitudes, high winds, storm seas and the heat of the sun in temperate or tropical latitudes.

So, how do seabirds deal with challenges such as the wind, water clarity or murkiness, ocean currents, the distribution of prey species and the ephemeral nature of concentrated food sources?

Wind is one of the most prominent factors in the life of a seabird, especially between 40 and 60 degrees latitude where it blows almost continually. Regular and strong westerlies prevail in this large swath of the Pacific from California to Alaska and in the Atlantic from the U.S. eastern seaboard to Newfoundland and Labrador. Species such as northern fulmars, shearwaters and albatrosses, which spend most of their lives foraging on the high seas in these latitudes, can travel great distances with a minimum of effort by taking advantage of the wind. They do this by using their long, slender wings to soar just above the waves, beating them only occasionally to maintain lift, thereby using less energy than would flapping flight. Of course, the wind isn't a boon to all seabirds or coastal birds. It can be a hindrance to species that haven't specifically adapted to forage in it, especially small, light birds such as storm-petrels and terns that are easily buffeted by strong winds. Waves and ripples created by the wind also make it difficult for plunge-diving birds to see prey beneath the surface.

Although water clarity doesn't affect birds that feed in very shallow water near the shore, it has determined the foraging habits of birds that feed in deeper water. Terns, brown pelicans, gannets and frigatebirds, all of them plunge divers, must be able to visually locate fish that are below the surface, so relatively clear water is required. These species avoid foraging in areas with murky water. On the other hand, birds that pursue their prey underwater, such as

Puffins foraging on the surface of the sea

cormorants and auks, may benefit from murky water as it enables them to use stealth and the element of surprise to capture prey.

Ocean currents are one of the most important factors affecting the distribution of marine life. Because of their impact on the overall global climate, water temperature and marine weather patterns, currents are crucial in determining where food is located in the ocean. Particularly important for seabirds are upwellings where deeper water is deflected toward the surface by a bottom feature such as the continental shelf, a seamount or a shoal. Fish and other prey species are carried from greater depths to the surface by this moving water, making them available as food. This is very important for seabirds, since they are unable to dive very deep while foraging. In fact, the very basis of the ocean food web, photosynthetic plankton, depends on nutrients brought to the surface by these upwellings. Tidal currents are also important factors in seabirds' foraging strategies, particularly near coastal breeding colonies. For example, certain species, such as black-legged kittiwakes in Alaska, will time their foraging trips with the tides.

Foraging range is determined by how far a bird must fly from its colony to find its prey species. Often, food supplies are found in the same general areas year after year. For instance, two of the most important fish for North American seabirds during the breeding season are the capelin and the sand lance, both of which are reliably found quite close to shore in the summer. At the other end of the spectrum are species like flying fish (and their eggs) or pelagic squid. These species can be extremely abundant and are a significant food resource for some seabirds, but it is impossible to predict where and when they will show up. To exploit practically every food resource available to them in the sea, seabirds and coastal birds have evolved into three main types of foragers:

- *Species that normally feed well offshore, on the "high seas" beyond the continental shelf.*

  This group includes storm-petrels, shearwaters, northern fulmars, horned and tufted puffins (both puffin species will travel great distances offshore during the non-breeding season), albatrosses and frigatebirds. Some birds, such as albatrosses and shearwaters, will breed on oceanic islands that are located a long distance from the mainland. Others, such as puffins, nest on inshore locations in the summer, then move offshore in the non-breeding season when the obligation to return to the nest each day to feed a hungry chick is behind them.

- *Species that feed in inshore environments.*
  Although they are often well out of sight of land, these species normally don't go beyond the continental shelf to feed and some may be found foraging in estuaries and bays. Most birds belonging to this group nest on inshore islands or along the coasts. Included in this group are cormorants, common eiders, northern gannets, most gulls, most terns, skimmers, brown pelicans and the auks.

- *Species that forage along the coast in the non-breeding season and normally breed inland.*
  Includes many of the shorebirds, grebes, loons, jaegers (though they may be found some distance offshore when not breeding), some gulls and most sea ducks.

Whether a seabird feeds at night or during the day depends on a number of factors. Most are visual foragers and seek out food during daylight hours. However, some will take advantage of a food supply whenever it is available. The black-legged kittiwakes in Alaska, for example, time their feeding with the tides. Certain populations of this species, as well as some populations of thick-billed murres, will feed on krill (a type of shrimp) that migrate to the surface only at night. Open-ocean birds like albatrosses, shearwaters and northern fulmars are thought to forage at night on surface-dwelling prey. Such birds may use an acute sense of smell (an unusual trait for birds) to locate prey in the dark.

Although few seabird species form groups while they *search* for food the way shorebirds do, the ephemeral nature of prey abundance in the oceans has resulted in a strong tendency for them to group at a feeding site once food has been found. As more and more birds join a feeding congregation at sea, the overall likelihood of any given individual capturing prey may actually increase as the large number of birds may disrupt the instinctive predator evasion techniques of fish. Of course, seabird species don't only gather together when one of their own finds food. They also congregate at prey found by other birds, as well as by whales, seals and sea lions.

A more "sinister" practice has evolved among some birds to exploit scarce food resources at sea. Frigatebirds, gulls, terns and jaegers have become pirates of the bird world, often stealing food that has been caught by other species. This practice is known as kleptoparasitism.

A common tern hovers before going into a dive

INTRODUCTION TO THE SPECIES ACCOUNTS

It is not enough to know how to simply identify a bird. Just as important, and perhaps even more so, is an understanding of the *way* it lives. What habitats does it prefer? How does it feed and get around? What does it sound like? What does it eat? How does it nest and rear its young? Does it migrate and, if so, when? Who are its closest relatives? And perhaps, the most important question of all in light of the increasing pressure being put on the ocean's ecosystems by humans: How healthy is its population?

There are fifty species in this book, a representative selection from the fifteen families in which seabirds and coastal birds are found. Every species account features photographs and range maps, as well as a natural history profile that is divided into nine sections. Each account is specific to the season in which the bird is most likely to be observed in the marine or coastal environment (of course, most are found in that environment *throughout* the year). For example, under the "Appearance" section in the common loon account, I first describe the wintering plumage, while the "Habitat" and "Behavior" sections primarily apply to the non-breeding season when the bird spends its time along the coast.

For some of the more threatened species a conservation status map is also included. The "Species Status Overall for North America" under the "Conservation Concerns" section for each species, as well as the range maps and conservation maps, are derived from NatureServe.org. This non-profit collaboration of Western Hemisphere conservation groups and agencies provides some of the most current and accurate data available to those working in the field of conservation biology.

The NatureServe species status definitions are as follows:

- Secure—*Common, widespread and abundant in the nation.*
- Apparently secure—*Uncommon, but not rare; some cause for long-term concern due to declines or other factors.*
- Vulnerable—*Vulnerable in the nation or state/province due to a restricted range, relatively few populations (often 80 or fewer), recent and widespread declines or other factors making it vulnerable to extirpation (localized extinction).*
- Imperiled—*Imperiled in the nation or state/province because of rarity due to very restricted range, very few populations (often 20 or fewer), steep declines or other factors making it vulnerable to extirpation from the nation or state/province.*
- Critically Imperiled—*Critically imperiled in the nation or state/province because of extreme rarity (often 5 or fewer occurrences) or because of some factor(s) such as very steep declines making it especially vulnerable to extirpation from the nation or state/province.*

A note about some other terminology in the species accounts:

- *Altricial* young are born helpless, without feathers or down, often with eyes closed, and are totally dependent on their parents.
- *Semi-altricial* young are born with eyes either open or closed and are down-covered but unable to leave the nest. They are completely dependent on parents.
- *Precocial* young are born with eyes open and covered in down, and are able to leave the nest within two days. They may be partially dependent or not dependent on parents to survive.
- *Pelagic* birds spend most of their lives on the open sea away from the coasts.
- *Monogamous pairs* mate only with one another in a breeding season. Some species have a long-term pair that may last several years or a lifetime.
- *Polygamous* mating occurs when both males and females may have two or more mates.
- *Polygynous* mating occurs when a male breeds with two or more mates.

RANGE MAP LEGEND

Permanent Resident	■	Breeding Resident	■
Non-breeding Resident	■	Passage Migrant	■
Uncertain Status	■	Introduced	■
Vagrant	■		

CONSERVATION MAP LEGEND

Presumed Extirpated	■	Possibly Extirpated	■
Critically Imperiled	■	Imperiled	■
Vulnerable	■	Apparently Secure	■
Secure	■	Not Ranked/ Under Review	■

SURFACE DIVERS

COMMON LOON

Gavia immer

During the non-breeding season, when most common loons spend their time along the coasts, they have a much plainer plumage

Though known primarily as a bird of the inland lakes where it nests, the common loon in fact spends more of its life on coastal waters than in freshwater.

APPEARANCE

Length 27–35 inches. Wingspan 50 inches. A large, heavy waterbird. In winter, dark above, light below. During the non-breeding season loons have a dark gray plumage above with whitish cheeks, throat, breast and undersides. Breeding plumage is black and white overall with a black head and neck. Bold white markings on the throat and lower sides of the thick, medium-length neck. Sexes look similar.

HABITAT

The range of the common loon

During the non-breeding season it frequents exposed ocean shorelines, estuaries, bays. Occasionally found wintering on open freshwater in more southern parts of its wintering range. During the breeding season the common loon generally inhabits mid- to northern-latitude lakes that have a large supply of prey and are large enough for the bird to take off and land. A suitable nesting site must also be available.

BEHAVIOR

Forages by swimming underwater using its large powerful legs and feet to propel itself as it pursues fish. Dives last up to a minute and loons have been known to reach a depth of nearly 200 feet. Prey is swallowed underwater. (Large prey is often taken to the surface to be swallowed.) Does not leave the water, except for flight and when on the nest. Flight is powerful, swift and direct on rapid, shallow wing beats. Requires a long, flapping run across the surface of the water to become airborne. Very strong surface swimmer. Extremely awkward on land, using its rear-set legs to push itself across the ground on its belly.

CALLS

Infrequently calls during the winter, except for occasional short hoots. In summer its main breeding calls include the "wail-call" given by both males and females to help locate one another. About 2 seconds in duration, it contains a distinct rise in pitch, sometimes ending on a lower note. The "tremolo-call," a short wavering note that lasts about half a second, is given at the appearance of an intruder or a disturbance. The "yodel-call" is a complex undulating call uttered by the male and usually signals territorial ownership.

FOOD

In coastal wintering areas it eats mainly fish, but also crabs and other marine invertebrates. During the breeding season it takes fish, crayfish, frogs, salamanders, leeches and aquatic insects.

FAMILY LIFE

Monogamous pair. Breeds exclusively on bodies of freshwater. Male and female build the nest, which is a mass of aquatic vegetation at the edge of the water. Usually located on a small island for protection from predators. The typical clutch of two eggs is incubated by both adults for 26 to 31 days. The precocial young leave the nest one day after the last egg has hatched and are

A common loon in winter plumage swallows a fish

tended and fed by both parents for 75 to 80 days. One brood per year, but a second brood is often attempted if the first one fails.

MIGRATION

Arrives on breeding lakes soon after ice breakup in March to June (the latter in more northerly areas). Fall migration occurs from September to December. First-year young do not migrate south with their parents, but winter in marine coastal areas that are farther north than those of adult birds.

CONSERVATION CONCERNS

Species status overall in North America is apparently secure in the United States (where it appears to be declining) and secure in Canada (where about 90 percent of the continent's common loons breed). Acid rain, industrial pollution (especially mercury), the ingestion of lead shot from the bottom of lakes, loss of nesting habitat along lake shores, and disturbance caused by boats have an impact on the loon's breeding success.

RELATED SPECIES

The common loon is one of four species of loons in North America, all belong to the genus *Gavia*.

HORNED GREBE

Podiceps auritus

The tiny horned grebe is found along both the Atlantic and Pacific coasts during winter

This little bird is sometimes easy to miss on its coastal winter range where its small size and dull coloration make it difficult to pick out among the tossing waves.

APPEARANCE

Length 14 inches. Wingspan 18 inches. A small diver, drably colored while on its wintering habitat. Dark gray-brown back, whitish neck and white cheek patch. Head appears relatively large and has a slightly peaked "bump" on the back. Short, light-colored bill and red eye. In summer the species is transformed into a beautiful rufous red with a dark back, a dark head with a large rakish yellow patch that forms somewhat of a crest in the back and a black bill.

HABITAT

In winter it is found generally along the Atlantic and Pacific coasts in sheltered bays and estuaries, usually near shore. Often seen in the same areas as wintering red-necked grebes and common loons. Occasionally found some distance from shore. Some birds also winter on larger bodies of freshwater. During the breeding season they are found on small, shallow freshwater ponds, marshes or lakes with emergent aquatic plants such as cattails and rushes.

The range of the horned grebe

BEHAVIOR

Forages by diving to fairly shallow depths to capture food. On marine wintering range it generally dives to capture prey located on the bottom. On breeding range will capture prey in mid-water. Dives are usually less than 30 seconds in length, but can last over a minute. During winter they are occasionally found in large feeding flocks of a hundred birds or more that may dive synchronously to pursue prey. Very efficient diver, propelling itself through the water with both feet kicking simultaneously. Generally holds its wings against its body while diving, but may use them to assist in rapid maneuvering. Strong surface swimmer. Flight is quick and direct on rapidly beating wings. A long run along the surface of the water is needed to get airborne. Rear-set legs result in awkward movement on land.

CALLS

Usually silent on its coastal wintering ground. Quite vocal on breeding grounds with a variety of trills, chatters, *kuk-kuks*, croaks and squeals.

FOOD

Diet on coastal wintering grounds includes a variety of small fish, crustaceans, marine worms and other invertebrates. In summer consumes mainly aquatic insects, crustaceans and mollusks, as well as capturing insects that fly near the surface of the water.

FAMILY LIFE

Monogamous pair. Breeds only on bodies of freshwater. Occasionally nests in small, loose colonies. Both sexes build a floating platform nest of aquatic plants, rotting vegetation and mud that is usually anchored to vegetation. The typical clutch of four to seven eggs is incubated for 22 to 25 days by both the male and female. The precocial young are fed and tended by both parents for 45 to 60 days. One brood per year, occasionally two.

MIGRATION

Spring migrants generally arrive on their breeding grounds from late April to late May. Fall migration usually occurs between late September and mid-November.

CONSERVATION CONCERNS

Species status overall in North America is secure in the United States and secure in Canada. Formerly hunted for their feathers for the millinery trade. Oil spills along its coastal wintering grounds are an ever-present threat.

RELATED SPECIES

One of seven grebe species in North America. The horned grebe shares its genus *Podiceps* with two other species, the red-necked grebe and the eared grebe.

Though quite striking during its breeding season when it is found inland on lakes, in winter, the horned grebe wears rather drab plumage

RED-NECKED GREBE

Podiceps grisegena

Red-necked grebes are often found in the same winter habitats—bays, harbors and occasionally open coast—as loons

This stubby-bodied, long-necked diver is reminiscent of a tiny loon as it swims and dives its way across sheltered ocean bays during the winter. Like the loon, it spends most of its year on salt water and breeds on inland bodies of water during the summer.

APPEARANCE
Length 18 inches. Wingspan 24 inches. In winter, red-necked grebes are rather drab with an overall dull brown plumage and a whitish chin, ear patch and collar. A very short tail gives the body a stubby appearance. Neck is relatively long compared to its short body. Bill is fairly long, chisel-shaped and yellow. Breeding plumage is much more colorful with a dark back, reddish brown neck, throat and breast, a black crown and a white cheek patch. During flight two white wing patches are visible. Appears very buoyant on the water.

HABITAT

Most of the population spends winters along the Atlantic and Pacific coasts of North America. Prefers inlets, bays and estuaries, but can often be found offshore over shallow feeding areas. A small part of the population winters on the Great Lakes. In summer, red-necked grebes prefer small, shallow freshwater ponds and lakes, protected bays of larger lakes, deep marshes, small sloughs and occasionally bogs and rivers.

The range of the red-necked grebe

BEHAVIOR

Forages by diving to capture prey on or near the bottom. May snap multiple small animals up in its bill during a single dive. Dives are usually about 30 seconds in length, but have been recorded at over 2 minutes. Begins a dive by either making a smooth submersion from the surface or springing into the water in an arcing motion. A very strong diver, it propels itself with its feet while holding its wings tightly against its body. Will generally swallow its prey underwater, but larger fish may be brought to the surface first. Also picks aquatic plants and food off surface of the water. Strong surface swimmer. Since it nests on a mat of floating vegetation, this bird rarely goes onto land and its rear-set legs make it extremely awkward when it does so. Flight is rapid on quickly beating wings. Needs a long take-off run along the water before getting airborne. It will fly very little outside of actual migration, preferring to spend its time on the water.

CALLS

Usually silent in winter and while migrating. During breeding and courtship season, however, red-necked grebes are a very noisy species and give a variety of braying, grunting and quacking sounds. Most commonly heard call is nasal *honk*.

FOOD

Diet consists mostly of small fish species such as eels, minnows and herring. Also takes shrimp, small crabs, prawns and other small marine invertebrates. On its freshwater breeding grounds it takes a wide variety of small fish, aquatic insects, other invertebrates and a small amount of plant matter.

FAMILY LIFE

Monogamous pair. Breeds exclusively on freshwater. Occasionally breeds in small colonies. Both male and female build the nest, which is a floating mass of soft aquatic plant material anchored in vegetation. Nest is placed either in the open or among reeds. The typical clutch of four to five eggs is incubated for 20 to 23 days by both sexes. Parents carry the precocial young on their backs until they learn to swim and dive. They are fed and tended by both parents for 49 to 70 days. One brood per year.

This red-necked grebe is beginning to show some of the red plumage that gives the species its name

MIGRATION

Spring migrants arrive on breeding grounds when ice breaks up between late April and mid-May. Adults leave breeding lakes to commence fall migration to marine areas between late July and mid-September.

CONSERVATION CONCERNS

Species status overall in North America is secure in the United States and secure in Canada. Red-necked grebes are susceptible to pollutants in their environment. Oil spills pose a particular threat on marine wintering grounds. Loss of breeding habitat caused by development and agriculture is a concern.

RELATED SPECIES

One of seven grebe species in North America. The red-necked grebe shares its genus *Podiceps* with two other species, the horned grebe and the eared grebe.

DOUBLE-CRESTED CORMORANT

Phalacrocorax auritus

The double-crested cormorant is the most widely distributed member of its family in North America

With a large and growing population, this familiar waterbird is one of the most frequently observed coastal species in North America.

APPEARANCE
Length 32 inches. Wingspan 52 inches. A large, all-black or dark brown bird, roughly similar in shape to a loon. The long, hooked bill is bright yellow. Cormorants float very low in the water with just the top of the back and the head and neck visible. The tail is completely submerged. The seldom-seen small, white head crests, for which the species is named, are somewhat more apparent in western birds.

The range of the double-crested cormorant

HABITAT

Generally found on saltwater bays, coves and estuaries, as well as along more exposed shores. Rarely strays far from the coast. Although largely a coastal bird, it has become quite abundant in some freshwater habitats such as the Great Lakes, as well as many smaller lakes, swamps, marshes and rivers. Double-crested cormorants will exploit a habitat as long as there is suitable food available, the water is deep enough and they have enough room to take off.

BEHAVIOR

Forages by diving underwater in pursuit of fish. Dives can last 30 seconds or longer. Very strong swimmer. Uses its large webbed feet for propulsion underwater. Brings fish to surface before eating. Flight is very strong and rapid on steady, strong wing beats. Must run across the water for some distance before getting airborne. Groups of double-crested cormorants are often seen flying in a V-formation. Regularly perches with its wings spread. This may be to dry the layer of insulating feathers against the skin. Awkward on land.

CALLS

Largely silent except near the nest where a variety of guttural croaking sounds are made during courtship.

FOOD

Fish are eaten almost exclusively. Various sizes and species are taken. Will occasionally take aquatic invertebrates.

FAMILY LIFE

Monogamous pair. Nests in colonies ranging from a few individuals to hundreds of birds, often mixing with nesting herons and egrets. Both male and female participate in building a platform nest of sticks and twigs, which is placed either on the ground or in a tree. Typical clutch of three to four eggs is incubated by both sexes for 28 days. Altricial young are fed regurgitated food by both parents for 35 to 42 days. One brood per year.

MIGRATION
Birds usually begin to arrive on the breeding grounds in March, with the peak migration during April and May. By October most of them will have left on the migration south. Many birds breeding in coastal areas are year-round residents.

CONSERVATION CONCERNS
Species status overall in North America is secure in the United States and secure in Canada. Despite having been decimated by DDT in the mid-twentieth century, the population of the double-crested cormorant is generally increasing across North America. However, many other cormorant species around the world are vulnerable to extinction.

RELATED SPECIES
There are six members of the cormorant family *Phalacrocoracidae* in North America.

Large webbed feet, characteristic of all cormorants, are evident on this perched double-crested cormorant

GREAT CORMORANT

Phalacrocorax carbo

The white side patch and shaggy crest of the great cormorant is evident here

One of the most widespread birds in the world, occurring on every continent except Antarctica. In the past, the world's largest cormorant was widely domesticated in Europe and Asia where it was trained to capture fish while wearing a collar with a retrieval line, a practice that continues in parts of China today. In North America, it is restricted to the Atlantic coast.

APPEARANCE
Length 36 inches. Wingspan 63 inches. A large black diving bird with a moderately stocky neck, a large head, a white throat patch and small yellow chin patch. During the breeding season it has a white "hip" patch on its side just below the wing. Though quite similar in appearance to the smaller double-crested cormorant, the two species can be told apart by the color of the throat patch, which is yellow on

the double-crested, and by the substantial difference in size. The juvenile great cormorant has a white belly and a brown neck. At a distance looks somewhat similar to the common loon, but generally floats lower and has a more crooked neck. Often seen perched near water on pilings, posts or rocks with its wings spread wide (whether the purpose of this stance is to dry the wings is not clear).

HABITAT

Although great cormorants throughout the rest of the world are generally birds of rivers and freshwater lakes, in North America they are almost exclusively marine and coastal in habit, preferring sheltered bays. Inhabit the rocky islands, cliffs and coasts of the North Atlantic. Rarely seen offshore. Occasionally feed in estuaries. Usually nest on cliff ledges or on islands that are free of predators.

The range of the great cormorant

BEHAVIOR

Forages by diving to the bottom in pursuit of fish. Sometimes dives to 100 feet. Propels itself with both feet simultaneously while holding its wings to the side. Will often travel some distance along the bottom before surfacing. Very quick and maneuverable underwater. Unlike many other species of waterbirds, cormorants' feathers will absorb some water, thus removing air and making the bird less buoyant and more efficient underwater. Appears to do deeper dives first to remove as much air as possible from feathers, thus reducing buoyancy and resulting in less energy used for subsequent dives. On the surface it is an efficient swimmer. Walks upright with a clumsy waddle on land; sometimes hops, but can move quite fast if necessary. Flight is powerful and fast on rapidly beating wings. Often alternates flapping and gliding. Must run along the water while flapping its wings to get airborne.

CALLS
Generally silent except on its nesting ground where it utters various guttural croaks and groans. Young give a high-pitched whining call.

FOOD
Eats fish almost exclusively. In North America, a large percentage of its diet is made up of bottom-dwelling fish such as sculpins, cunners, flounder and gunnels, as well as mid-water species including pollock and sand lance, among others. Occasionally takes small crustaceans such as crabs.

Great cormorants rest on a rock during a North Atlantic winter

FAMILY LIFE

Monogamous pair. Colonial breeding, often in mixed colonies with double-crested cormorants. Both adults build a large nest of sticks, twigs, seaweed, bits of garbage, fishing twine and grasses, lined with fine material. Nest normally placed on a cliff ledge. Known to occasionally nest in low shrubby trees. The typical clutch of four to five eggs is incubated by both sexes for 29 to 31 days. Altricial young are fed by both adults until they leave the nest at 50 days. One brood per year.

MIGRATION

Migration pattern not well known. Appears that some populations do not migrate but winter in the vicinity of their breeding grounds, perhaps dispersing somewhat to find food. Immature birds are more likely to migrate south, usually in late summer or early fall. Spring migrant birds apparently arrive on their breeding grounds in April or May, though many colony sites are occupied in March before the snow has melted.

CONSERVATION CONCERNS

Species status overall in North America is critically endangered in the United States because the species breeds only in very limited numbers exclusively in the state of Maine. Status for Canada is apparently secure. Its limited breeding range on the continent and the fact that it must compete with the much more abundant double-crested cormorant has kept great cormorant numbers relatively low.

RELATED SPECIES

One of six species of cormorants belonging to the genus *Phalacrocorax* in North America.

TUBE-NOSED
SEABIRDS

BLACK-FOOTED ALBATROSS

Phoebastria nigripes

The black-footed albatross, the most commonly observed albatross along the west coast of the continent, is one of the darkest in its family

Although it breeds only on isolated islands in the mid-Pacific, this dark-plumaged bird is the most commonly seen albatross along the west coast of North America, especially during the late spring and summer.

APPEARANCE

Length 32 inches. Wingspan 80 inches. An enormous seabird, somewhat gull-like in overall shape. Uniform, slightly mottled gray-brown plumage covers the body. Some birds show various lighter patches. Whitish gray area around the face. Bill is very large and dark, with a hooked tip. Legs and feet are black.

HABITAT

Like all albatrosses this is a true mariner, never setting foot on land except briefly to breed. It spends most of its life ranging over thousands of miles of the vast North Pacific. Breeds on isolated islands of the Hawaiian archipelago, such as Midway Island.

The range of the black-footed albatross

BEHAVIOR

Soars close to the water over vast stretches of the ocean in search of prey, often reaching the coast of western North America. Locates prey by sight as well as by using its tremendous sense of smell. Forages at the surface either by "tipping" and lowering the bill into the water like a duck or partly submerging its body to grab food. Will snatch flying fish from the air as it floats on the water, or will retrieve them after they enter the water. Follows fishing boats that are dumping fish offal into the sea. When swimming it floats quite high in the water and uses its very large webbed feet for propulsion. Flight is graceful on very long, slender wings. Performs dynamic and slope soaring, techniques that take advantage of the lift created by the wind flowing over the sea surface as well as up the slopes of waves. Can glide for hours in this way without flapping its wings. Must run along the surface to gain enough lift to get airborne.

CALLS

Utters a variety of squeals and grunts (the most common being a low *haw-haw*) when in the presence of other birds at sea or on its nesting ground. Will squeal as it approaches prey at sea.

FOOD

Diet is made up primarily of the eggs of flying fish, but also includes flying fish themselves, squid and crustaceans such as shrimp. Also consumes offal from fishing boats.

FAMILY LIFE
Monogamous pair that mates for life. Nests in colonies on the sand dunes of extremely isolated oceanic islands in the Pacific. Probably doesn't breed until 5 years old. Nest is a simple scrape in the sand. The single large egg is incubated by both sexes for 63 to 68 days. The semi-altricial chick stays in the nest for 140 to 150 days and is fed by both parents. One brood per year.

MIGRATION
After breeding, most birds migrate thousands of miles to the south in July and return north to breeding grounds in October or November.

CONSERVATION CONCERNS
Doesn't breed on the North American continent but is a regular visitor off the West Coast, especially during the non-breeding season. It is listed as endangered by the IUCN and is declining rapidly. At least 3,000 of the 100,000 total population of birds die annually while trying to retrieve the bait on longlines, where they get hooked and subsequently drown. Other threats include introduced predators on breeding islands, which prey on eggs and small young.

RELATED SPECIES
Most closely related to the Laysan and short-tailed albatrosses, which also belong to the genus *Phoebastria*.

Did You Know?
Seabirds such as albatrosses, shearwaters, fulmars and storm-petrels are known as "tube-noses." They possess very large nostrils that protrude from the top of the bill in a horny tube. These species have a highly acute sense of smell that allows them to use scent to find food over vast areas of the sea, as well as other individuals of their species, breeding areas, nesting sites and their young. This group of birds is unusual in that its species produces one chick per breeding season. Although only one chick is born to each pair, its survival rate is high, since adults invest a lot of time rearing it.

NORTHERN FULMAR

Fulmarus glacialis

Although it looks like a gull, the northern fulmar belongs to an entirely separate family of birds; unlike a gull, it is a true seabird that only comes to land to breed

Though similar in size and superficially similar in appearance to many gull species, the northern fulmar belongs to the same family of "tube-nosed" seabirds as the petrels and shearwaters. Although Charles Darwin erroneously considered it to be the most abundant bird species in the world, it nevertheless has a very large population.

APPEARANCE
Length 18 inches. Wingspan 42 inches. Wings are slender and the body is husky. Large, rounded head and thick neck. There are several color morphs of this species, but the most common is overall white with gray areas on the top of wings and the end of the tail. Other morphs may be gray overall or any combination of gray and white. Bill is short, heavy and hooked on the end with a small tube

on top that houses the nasal passages from whence salt is excreted. Easily distinguished from gulls at a distance by its stiff, shallow wing beats. Legs are placed far back on body.

HABITAT

Found well offshore throughout the Northern Hemisphere in predominantly ice-bound regions of the Arctic. Also inhabits sub-Arctic and northern temperate regions, but rarely moves south of these areas. Lives far from land except during nesting season. Breeds on precipitous sea cliffs on northern islands or mainland headlands and occasionally on small islets. Especially abundant in the Canadian Arctic and Alaska.

The range of the northern fulmar

BEHAVIOR

All foraging done from the surface of the water. Very buoyant swimmer. Prey usually captured by dipping the bill to grab food off the water's surface, plunging the head just beneath the surface, and by making shallow plunge dives to pursue prey. Unable to capture prey on the wing. Also an effective scavenger, consuming offal produced by fishing or whaling operations. This abundant resource supplied by the large fishing fleets in the northern oceans may be the reason the fulmar's population has experienced such a dramatic increase in recent times. Acute sense of smell is used to locate food. Often feeds at night. Sometimes called a "foul-gull" because of its nasty habit of "spitting" its rank, oily stomach contents at anything it sees to be a threat, whether another bird or a human handling it. The oily discharge often destroys the water-proofing in the targeted bird's feathers, sometimes resulting in its death. Flight is a combination of shallow, stiff flapping followed by glides, usually only 5 to 10 feet above the waves. Will often follow ships on the open ocean. Very adept at using updrafts and air currents as it soars and wheels gracefully in flight near the cliffs of its breeding colony. Very awkward on land due to extremely rear-set legs.

CALLS
Utters a variety of low grunts, cackles and clucks, usually while feeding or when on its breeding grounds.

FOOD
Opportunistic feeder that takes many species of small fish, squid and octopus, as well as invertebrates such as shrimp and jellyfish. Also commonly consumes offal and scavenges floating dead marine mammals such as whales, seals and walruses. In the Pacific, fulmars are known to capture bottom-dwelling crustaceans that have been stirred to the surface by foraging gray whales.

This northern fulmar is perched on a ledge at its breeding colony in the North Atlantic

FAMILY LIFE
Monogamous pair. Breeds in colonies located on islands or on mainland headlands. Nocturnal on breeding grounds. The lightly lined nest is either a scrape placed on a grassy shelf on a sea cliff, or a shallow depression placed on the ground. It is not known whether only one or both adults participate in nest building. The single egg is incubated by both adults for 50 to 60 days. The semi-altricial chick is fed by both parents for 46 to 51 days. One brood per season. Fulmars normally don't mate until they are 8 to 10 years old and only produce one egg per

year. Non-incubating or non-brooding members of the pair will take long trips of up to 4 to 5 days and may travel hundreds of miles from the colony to capture food for the chick. With an average life span of over 30 years, and with some individuals living for over 40 years, fulmars are one of the longest-lived birds.

MIGRATION
Does not migrate in any one direction per se, but simply disperses over the ocean at the end of the breeding season, which usually occurs in late summer to mid-October. Spring birds usually arrive at breeding sites in the high Arctic in late April to early May.

CONSERVATION CONCERNS
Species status overall in North America is apparently secure in the United States and secure in Canada. All breeding colonies in the United States are in Alaska and are located in the National Wildlife Refuge system. Canadian colonies receive little protection. Recent history has seen an increase in the population of the northern fulmar throughout much of its range, possibly due to the increased food supply provided by waste products of the fishing industry. However, the increasing rate of oil exploration in the Arctic and the fulmar's habit of congregating in relatively few large nesting colonies means the species is vulnerable to potential large-scale environmental disasters such as oil spills.

RELATED SPECIES
A member of the *Procellariidae* family of petrels and shearwaters, the northern fulmar shares its genus *Fulmarus* with only one other species, the very similar southern fulmar of southern polar oceans.

SOOTY SHEARWATER

Puffinus griseus

The sooty shearwater is one of the most widely ranging seabirds in the Northern Hemisphere

One of the most abundant seabirds in the world with an estimated 20 million individuals, this long-lived bird, which can live for over 30 years, is widely distributed over the world's oceans during the non-breeding season (the Northern Hemisphere summer). Though it breeds exclusively in the Southern Hemisphere in New Zealand, southern Chile, the Falkland Islands and Australia, it is one of the most commonly observed shearwater species along both the Atlantic and Pacific coasts of North America during late spring to early summer.

APPEARANCE
Length 17 inches. Wingspan 41 inches. From a distance it is a some-what gull-like, overall dark, "sooty" brown bird. Wings are long, slender and pointed with a panel of whitish gray on the undersides.

Bill is long, thin and dark and, if observed at close range, the "tube" that excretes salt can be seen on the top of the bill. Legs and feet are black. Distinguished from gulls at a distance by its stiff, fast wing beats.

HABITAT

Exclusively marine. Generally stays well offshore. In North American waters it is seen more often near the coast (occasionally seen from shore) than other shearwaters. As it follows oceanic food supplies it often associates with other species, such as the

The range of the sooty shearwater

greater shearwater in the Atlantic and the Buller's in the Pacific. Breeds on islands in the southern Pacific Ocean.

BEHAVIOR

Travels great distances over the sea in search of food. While swimming, it forages by seizing food on the surface or by bill-dipping prey from just beneath the surface of the water. Often follows whales to capture the fish they stir up at the surface; also follows fishing boats that are discarding offal. Occasionally dives to pursue prey underwater. The sooty shearwater is known to dive to an average maximum depth of over 120 feet. Short plunge dives from heights of 3 to 10 feet above the water are known to occur. Gathers in large flocks when a significant supply of food is found; in these circumstances it often associates with other seabird species. Flight is on stiff, shallow-beating wings, alternated with gliding. Bird will tilt from side to side, appearing to almost slice the surface of the water with its wing tip, hence the name shearwater. Performs dynamic soaring like an albatross to take advantage of air currents near the sea's surface. Must patter along the surface before becoming airborne.

CALLS
When competing for food at sea will often give noisy nasal squeals. Quite vocal on breeding colony, performing a range of low, guttural cooing and croaking calls.

FOOD
Diet consists primarily of small fish, squid and crustaceans.

FAMILY LIFE
Breeds in colonies, some very large. Birds don't breed until they are 5 to 7 years old. Ground burrow nest is lined with plant matter and is located in a chamber at the end of a tunnel that is up to 10 feet long. The single egg is incubated by both sexes for 52 to 56 days. Semi-altricial chick remains in the nest for over 90 days and will make first flight at about 100 days. Fed by both parents during this time. One brood per year.

MIGRATION
One of the widest ranging species on Earth. In the Atlantic, it migrates some 9,000 miles from breeding colonies near the southern tip of South America to Arctic waters in the Northern Hemisphere. Similar distances are covered in the Pacific. Recent experiments on tagged New Zealand birds showed that in one year they traveled about 46,000 miles in a huge figure eight over the Pacific.

CONSERVATION CONCERNS
Species status overall in North America is secure in the United States and secure in Canada. Although it is an abundant bird, declines have been observed. The cause of the decline is not known but global climate change is thought to possibly play a role.

RELATED SPECIES
The most commonly seen of nine species of shearwaters belonging to the genus *Puffinus* that regularly occur in North American waters.

FOOD

A wide variety of small food items found on the ocean's surface are taken by this opportunistic feeder. Small fish, squid, octopus and jellyfish, as well as shrimp and other crustaceans, are included in its diet. Also feeds on the oil left by the floating carcasses of whales and on whale feces. The petrel converts its food into a rich oil that is stored internally for later feeding to its chick.

A robin-sized Leach's storm-petrel, pattering along the water as it looks for prey

FAMILY LIFE

Monogamous pair. Colonies are located exclusively on islands. Nocturnal on breeding grounds. Males (and possibly rarely both adults) excavate a 1- to 3-foot-long burrow in a grassy slope, bank or occasionally among stumps or rocks. The burrow ends in an enlarged chamber padded with dry vegetation where the egg is laid and incubated. Only one egg laid and it is incubated by both adults for 38 to 46 days. Each adult will do a three-day non-stop incubation stint on the egg during which they may lose one-tenth of their body weight. Semi-altricial chick remains in the nest between 60 and 70 days and is fed nutritious regurgitated oil by both parents. One brood per year; occasionally a second egg is laid if the first fails.

MIGRATION

Once the brief summer breeding season is over, Leach's storm-petrels will not visit land for the rest of the year. Despite nesting throughout the Northern Hemisphere, they appear to spend their winters throughout the tropics. Spring migrants generally arrive on their breeding grounds between March and May. Fall migration usually occurs from early September to late October.

CONSERVATION CONCERNS

Species status overall in North America is secure in the United States and apparently secure in Canada. Its large population suggests that the species is healthy overall, however it is vulnerable to environmental contaminants such as oil spills, pesticides and heavy metals. Cats and rats, or other species that are introduced deliberately or accidentally to islands, can destroy entire petrel breeding colonies.

A conservation status map for the Leach's storm-petrel

RELATED SPECIES

Six other species belonging to the genus *Oceanodroma* are found in the oceans surrounding North America. As well, the Wilson's storm-petrel, an often-observed species that belongs to a different genus, is very similar in appearance.

Did You Know?

Certain birds that spend most of their lives at sea, and come to land only to breed, have special "salt glands" which enable them to remove the excess salt they ingest while they eat marine prey and drink seawater to maintain their water balance. These glands remove the salt from seawater, resulting in the excretion of a concentrated salt solution from the bird's nostrils. How these wonderful "filters" work is still a mystery to science.

LARGE AERIAL WATERBIRDS

NORTHERN GANNET

Morus bassanus

A northern gannet soaring majestically on its six foot wingspan

Nothing in the avian world is more thrilling to watch than the northern gannet as it plummets like a javelin from 100 feet in the air into a school of fish. The largest of the world's plunge divers, it breeds at six colonies in North America: three in the Atlantic around the island of Newfoundland and three in the Gulf of St. Lawrence.

APPEARANCE
Length 38 inches. Wingspan 72 inches. A very large, overall brilliant-white bird with long slender wings that have unmistakable, pointed black tips. Quite long and heavy pale blue bill tapers to a point; long tail also tapers to a point. Head of adult is light golden-brown to dull orange. Icy blue eyes are surrounded by a small black mask. Legs and feet are dark gray or black with light stripes running down tops of the toes. In flight the black wing tips, brilliant white plumage and

The range of the
northern gannet

cross-shaped form are diagnostic. Birds younger than 4 or 5 years have a mottled light and dark plumage.

HABITAT

During the majority of the year (the non-breeding season) the gannet doesn't touch down on land and is usually found around relatively shallow coastal waters inside the continental shelf. Rarely seen more than a few hundred miles from the coast. Often observed from shore foraging for fish. During the breeding season it generally stays within 40 miles of the coast. Breeding sites are usually located on the tops of sea stacks, on cliff ledges and at the edge of steep banks or cliffs on islands or headlands. Such places are chosen for their proximity to food and for protection from mammalian predators such as foxes.

BEHAVIOR

Forages by plunge diving into the ocean, sometimes from a great height, to capture fish near the surface. Often feeds in flocks. Enters the sea head-first with its wings pulled rearward behind its body at speeds of over 60 miles per hour. Will generally penetrate 10 to 20 feet below the surface, during which time it may capture a fish in its bill. Occasionally, by using its feet and wings to propel itself underwater, a gannet will swim up to 50 feet beneath the surface in pursuit of prey and may remain submerged for 30 seconds. Usually swallows prey underwater, though it will sometimes handle it briefly at the surface and swallow it before taking flight. Also feeds by pecking at food while swimming on the surface as well as diving from the surface. Not known to hunt at night. Flight is powerful and direct with quick wing beats followed by short glides, usually between 30 and 100 feet above the surface. Stands upright while walking but has an awkward waddling gait.

CALLS
An individual's call at the breeding colony is a harsh, guttural gargling *kor-ruck, kor-ruck, kor-ruck*. A large colony of thousands of birds produce a deafening cacophony. Generally silent when not at the breeding colony.

FOOD
Will eat almost any appropriately sized prey found at or just beneath the surface. A variety of species are taken including mackerel, short-finned squid, herring, capelin, menhaden, pollock and smelt, among others. Shrimp and other invertebrates also taken.

FAMILY LIFE
Monogamous pair; generally mates for life. Nests in large, raucous colonies located on islands or headlands. Male and female build a crude nest of seaweed, sticks, grass and flotsam that is placed on a ledge, slope or top of a sea stack. A complex mating "dance" is performed by the male and female at the nest site. A single egg is incubated by both adults for 42 to 44 days. The chick is fed regurgitated food by both parents until it leaves the nest after 95 to 107 days. One brood per year.

MIGRATION
Birds range widely along the east coast of North America during winter. Spring migrants generally arrive on breeding grounds in April. In fall, adults may fly north to feed off the

A northern gannet perched at its nesting colony

coast of Labrador before beginning their migration southward along the Atlantic coast.

CONSERVATION CONCERNS
Species status overall in North America is apparently secure in Canada (does not breed in the United States). Population is increasing. All nesting colonies in Canada are protected except one. However, as a top predator of relatively large fish, gannets tend to accumulate toxins such as PCBs in their bodies. The effect of this on the health of the birds is not known.

RELATED SPECIES
Although the northern gannet is the sole member of the genus *Morus*, the brown and masked boobies that are found in southern North American waters belong to the same family, *Sulidae*.

This northern gannet is in flight over its nesting colony, which is located on a precipitous sea stack

AMERICAN WHITE PELICAN

Pelecanus erythrorhynchos

Despite its distinction as one of the heaviest birds, the white pelican is graceful in flight

This magnificent species is the largest and one of the heaviest birds in North America.

APPEARANCE
Length 62 inches. Wingspan 108 inches. Weight 16 pounds. Unmistakably large white bird with an enormous orange-yellow bill and pouch. Short orange-yellow legs. In flight the trailing part of the wing and the wing tip are conspicuously black. Holds its neck in a slight "S" with head drawn back so that the heavy head and bill can be supported on the breast.

HABITAT
Generally winters in saltwater coastal areas, such as the shallow lagoons and estuaries that are found along the Gulf Coast and

The range of the American white pelican

California. Does not frequent deeper waters since it can't dive to capture food (unlike the brown pelican). Breeds on islands in freshwater lakes and rivers in the western part of the continent. Breeds in areas that are free of mammalian predators.

BEHAVIOR

Forages alone or in small flocks by scooping fish out of the water, often working cooperatively in a group. Once a school of fish is located, the group will gather in a line a short distance from the shore and will herd the fish into shallower water by beating the surface with their wings. Once they're shallow enough, the birds scoop the fish up, drain up to

An American white pelican takes off from the water

2 gallons of water from their pouches, then swallow their meal. Because of its positive buoyancy, it does not dive like the brown pelican. Flight is powerful and graceful with strong, relatively slow wing beats. An expert at soaring, it is often seen high in the sky as it circles on thermals. Though it is heavy and moves in a labored manner on land, its legs are well centered for walking.

CALLS

Silent, except on its breeding colony where it performs guttural croaks and grunts.

FOOD
Diet consists almost entirely of fish, but will also eat crustaceans such as crabs.

American white pelicans cooperatively feed

FAMILY LIFE
Monogamous pair. Nests exclusively in dense colonies on flat islands or on shorelines of bodies of freshwater. Both sexes excavate a scrape in the earth and use surrounding dirt, plant stems, bits of wood and other fine material to create a rim around the eggs. The typical clutch of two eggs is incubated by both sexes. Altricial young are fed by both parents for at least 60 days. The younger bird in brood usually starves to death due to harassment by its older sibling. One brood per year.

MIGRATION
Entire population is migratory. Birds migrate to inland breeding areas in the north-central interior of the continent in spring and move to coastal wintering areas (as well as freshwater lakes) in southern parts of the continent and southward to Central America.

CONSERVATION CONCERNS
Overall species status in North America is vulnerable in the United States and apparently secure in Canada where the majority of the species' seventy or so breeding colonies are located. Shooting by humans continues to be a major cause of mortality. Although the population may be increasing overall, most of its breeding colonies are highly vulnerable to fluctuating water levels due to drought and dams. Low water levels improve access for mammals that prey on the eggs, reducing the pelican's reproductive success. Because it must fish in very shallow water on its coastal wintering grounds, changing sea levels and fish distributions brought about by global warming may have a negative impact on the species.

RELATED SPECIES
The other North American pelican species that shares the genus *Pelecanus* is the brown pelican.

BROWN PELICAN

Pelecanus occidentalis

A brown pelican skims over the sea

The graceful flight of this amazing aviator belies the bird's large size as it skims so close to the sea that it practically touches the water with its wing tips.

APPEARANCE

Length 51 inches. Wingspan 79 inches. World's smallest pelican. A large bird with a streaked silvery-brown back, extremely large whitish head with a yellow forecrown and an enormous bill, similar in shape to the white pelican's. White and dark brown striped neck; blackish brown breast and underparts. Short gray legs. At a distance appears much darker overall than the white pelican. In flight neck is an "S" shape with the head drawn into the body where it is supported on the breast.

The range of the brown pelican

HABITAT

Found along the more southerly Atlantic and Pacific coasts and around the Gulf of Mexico where it feeds in clear waters. Often rests in estuaries and lagoons. Breeds on open coastal islands. Rarely seen inland, except in California's Salton Sea where it is common.

BEHAVIOR

Spectacular foraging technique. On spotting a fish while patrolling over water at an altitude of 30 feet or so, the brown pelican will turn sharply and head into a vertical dive with its bill thrust forward and its wings half folded behind it. It hits the water with a great splash and is carried beneath the surface, its bill open wide to scoop up any unfortunate fish in its path. Brown pelicans are often harassed by gulls, and fish are sometimes pirated from them by terns. Flight is powerful with strong wing beats alternating with short glides. Often flies in single file in groups, gliding for long distances on the momentum gained from updrafts created by the waves. Spends much time floating on the surface and is a good swimmer. Moves about on land with relative efficiency.

A conservation map for the brown pelican

CALLS

Largely silent except for some low clucking. Young birds on the breeding ground are more vocal.

FOOD

Diet largely consists of fish such as menhaden and anchovies, but also consumes free-swimming crustaceans such as prawns and shrimp.

FAMILY LIFE

Monogamous pair. Colonial nester. Both sexes participate in building a nest of sticks, twigs, reeds and grasses on the ground or in the tops of low brushy trees such as mangroves. Tree nests tend to be more elaborate than the ground nests, which may be little more than a scrape in the earth. The typical clutch of three eggs is incubated by both adults for 28 to 30 days. Altricial young are tended and fed by both parents for 71 to 88 days until they fledge. One brood per year.

MIGRATION

Birds breeding in more northerly parts of the range along the Atlantic and Pacific coasts will winter along the southern coasts of North America, as well as in Central and South America.

CONSERVATION CONCERNS

Overall status in North America is apparently secure in the United States. Still listed as an endangered or threatened species in parts of the United States. Population crashed in the mid-twentieth century due to eggshell thinning brought on by widespread pesticide use. Population is recovering.

RELATED SPECIES

The other pelican in North America is the American white pelican, also of the genus *Pelecanus*.

A brown pelican preening its feathers

MAGNIFICENT FRIGATEBIRD

Fregata magnificens

A male magnificent frigatebird inflates its throat sac during breeding season

This graceful, large seabird sails effortlessly along the southern coasts of North America on its long, pointed wings, sometimes with nary a wing beat for hours.

APPEARANCE
Length 40 inches. Wingspan 90 inches. A very large, slender bird that is somewhat fantastical in appearance. Has the largest wingspan relative to its weight of any bird. Black overall. Wings are long, pointed and very angular with a distinctive bend in the middle. Deeply forked tail is extremely long and often folded into a point. Body is largely black, except for a white patch on the female's breast and shoulders. Bill is long, thin and relatively straight with a large hook at the end. Legs and feet (rarely seen) are relatively small, weak and pinkish.

Male has a red gular (throat) sac that it inflates to balloon-like size during sexual displays.

HABITAT

Inhabits tropical to temperate seas; generally not observed far offshore. Usually seen patrolling along the coast in areas where large fish pursue the schools of smaller fish that are potential prey for the frigatebird. Often found where other marine birds such as terns, gulls and pelicans congregate for feeding. Does not land on the water and roosts on land at the coast, usually in mangrove forests.

The range of the magnificent frigatebird

BEHAVIOR

After spotting a potential meal from altitude with its acute eyesight, it uses precise timing and coordination first to dive, then to swoop very close to the water. There, while still on the wing, it uses its long, hooked bill to grab prey from just above (in the case of flying fish), on or just below the surface. Then it continues its flight, having never landed on the water. Scavenges offal and other animal waste at sea in the same way. Becomes helpless if it alights on water, and is unable to take off. Also harasses other large marine birds such as pelicans and cormorants in order to force them to drop their catch, which is then grabbed in mid-air by the frigatebird (also known as the *man-o-war* bird for these piratical tendencies). Flight is buoyant, graceful and very agile on very large wings. An expert at soaring on thermals.

CALLS

The male has a shrill howling call, as well as harsh rattling and gurgling notes while on its breeding grounds.

This female magnificent frigatebird in flight shows how large its wings are relative to its body and just how deeply forked its long tail is

FOOD

Diet includes fish (generally 12 inches long or more), large jellyfish, crustaceans and other invertebrates, offal and occasionally baby sea turtles.

FAMILY LIFE

Monogamous pair. Breeds in colonies. Both sexes participate in building a shallow platform nest of sticks, twigs and grass that is located in a mangrove, a tree or a bush. The single egg is incubated for 40 to 50 days by both adults. The altricial young is fed and tended by both parents for up to 6 months. Females generally breed only once every 2 years.

MIGRATION

Generally non-migratory, but birds may wander large distances in search of food, particularly during the non-breeding season.

CONSERVATION CONCERNS

Species status overall for North America is apparently secure for the United States where it is for the most part a non-breeder. In Florida, where a small colony (the only one in the U.S.) breeds on the Dry Tortugas, the bird is considered critically imperiled. A tropical bird, it is much more common south of the U.S.

RELATED SPECIES

The magnificent is the only species of frigatebird usually observed in North America. There are four other species of frigatebird worldwide—the great, lesser, Ascension Island and Christmas

Island frigatebirds—the last two threatened species due to their small ranges. All five belong to the genus *Fregata*.

Did You Know?

The clutch size (the number of eggs laid) of various species of birds varies widely from large aggregations of ten eggs or more in ground-nesting forest and upland birds like pheasants, grouse and quail, to the single egg of many seabird species. The key concept here is not how many eggs a female will lay in a season, but how many she will lay over a lifetime. Birds that lay many eggs per year tend to be relatively short-lived, while those that produce one or only a few eggs per year tend to have greater life spans, so the overall number produced in a lifetime will be roughly the same. Birds with fewer eggs also tend to invest more time in rearing the chick, resulting in a fairly high rate of survival.

DUCKS AND GEESE

BRANT

Branta bernicla

A brant wades through rockweed as it searches for food along the Atlantic coast

Smaller and less vocal than its noisy, ubiquitous cousin the Canada goose, the brant, scarcely larger than a black duck, is a goose with a rather limited range that winters along both of North America's coasts.

APPEARANCE
Length 24 inches. Wingspan 44 inches. A small goose with a short neck and a small bill. Neck, head, throat and breast are black; head lacks the white cheek patch of the Canada goose. Tail is black but is partially covered by white covert feathers. Small, but conspicuous white "necklace" doesn't quite encircle the front of the neck on the eastern brant but does on the darker western form. Dark gray back and a lighter gray belly (except on western "black" brant which has a dark gray belly).

HABITAT

The range of the brant

The most exclusively marine of North American geese. Spends its winters along both the Atlantic and Pacific coasts. Favors shallow intertidal areas with mudflats where an abundance of easily reached vegetation such as marine grasses and sea lettuce are available. Will often choose areas behind barrier beaches for protection from the weather. On some wintering areas will occasionally move from the water and feed in short-grass salt marshes. Rarely, brant may be found feeding on golf courses and other groomed grassy places in more populated areas within their wintering range. Habitat during the breeding season is along the landward edges of Arctic salt marshes, around river deltas, along shallow braided streams, on low coasts and islands, as well as on freshwater lakes.

BEHAVIOR

Forages in the typical style of a goose by swimming through the shallows and dipping its head in the water. Will also tip its body forward to reach deeper food. Occasionally picks bits of food off the water's surface. Also walks on intertidal flats, shorelines or grassy areas (especially in Arctic breeding grounds) to graze for food. An efficient walker with legs well placed for agile movement on land. Though it spends much time swimming, it is not as powerful a swimmer on the surface as many sea ducks, and generally avoids areas of current. Flight is strong and direct with powerful wing beats. A group in flight forms a straight line and does not fly in a "V" like many other goose species.

CALLS

Call is a drawn-out, hoarse *cronk*. Also utters a variety of soft grunts and hisses.

Brant geese in flight look similar to Canada geese

FOOD

Primary food item while on wintering grounds is the eel-grass that is found in intertidal areas. This heavy reliance on one key native plant makes the species vulnerable to food shortages when the eel-grass is in short supply. Also consumes sea lettuce, green algae, surf grass, cordgrass and other plants. Occasionally eats small marine invertebrates. On its breeding ground the brant eats mostly aquatic plants, sedges, marsh grasses and mosses among other vegetation. Some animal food, such as insects and their larvae, are taken as well.

FAMILY LIFE

Monogamous pair. Occasionally forms loose colonies. Female builds a shallow bowl-shaped nest of seaweed, moss and lichen, lined with down. Nest is placed on the ground, usually near water on a small island in a lake or pond on the Arctic tundra, or in a river delta. Nest generally located within several miles of the coast. The reduction in Arctic fox numbers has reduced their predation on the brant, which has made nesting on mainland areas more viable. The typical clutch of three to five eggs is incubated for 22 to 26 days by the female. Precocial young leave the nest soon after hatching and are soon able to feed themselves, but they are tended by both parents for 40 to 50 days. One brood per year.

MIGRATION
Brant have one of the longest migrations of any North American waterfowl species, nesting in the high Arctic and wintering as far south as Baja, Mexico, on the west coast and North Carolina on the east coast. North American breeding birds also winter in parts of northern Europe (birds that winter in the UK migrate across the Greenland ice cap on their way to breeding grounds in the eastern Canadian Arctic). Spring migrants begin arriving on breeding grounds in late April and early May in parts of the western Arctic mainland and early June in the high Arctic islands. Fall migration generally occurs from September to early October. Partway through their southward migration, birds will stop at a staging area (location depends on where in the Arctic they breed) where eel-grass is plentiful before continuing to wintering areas.

CONSERVATION CONCERNS
Species status overall in North America is secure in the United States and secure in Canada. As a migrant it is listed as only apparently secure in Canada, meaning that certain populations that do not breed in Canada may face threats as they migrate through or winter in Canada. The brant nearly became extinct in the 1930s when eel-grass, its primary food source, suffered a global die-off. The result of this was hard on all species that depended on the grass, and the eel-grass limpet, a marine snail-like animal, became extinct. Luckily, brant were eventually able to adapt to eating other plants to supplement their diet. Eel-grass has made somewhat of a comeback while brant have continued to eat other species of vegetation, such as sea lettuce.

RELATED SPECIES
The brant, Canada goose and the cackling goose all belong to the genus *Branta*.

GREATER SCAUP
Aythya marila

Male greater scaup wintering on a calm bay

One of the most widely distributed ducks worldwide, the greater scaup is circumpolar in range, occurring in both the Eastern and Western Hemispheres. Relatively little is known about it, owing to its habit of breeding in remote, isolated areas.

APPEARANCE
Length 18 inches. Wingspan 28 inches. A relatively large duck with a large head. From a distance, male appears black and white overall; only upon closer inspection does the glossy greenish tinge of its head become apparent. Head, neck, throat and breast are dark. Bill is blue-gray with a black tip. Sides are light and tail is blackish; back is gray. Female is dull brown overall with white around the base of the bill. Light gray to white underside of wings on both sexes. Often seen in large flocks.

HABITAT

The majority of its year is spent on coastal marine waters in ice-free protected shallow bays and inlets, as well as estuaries. Generally avoids coastal currents. During the breeding season it is found on shallow lakes and ponds.

The range of the greater scaup

BEHAVIOR

Forages by taking shallow dives to gather food items from the soft sediments on the bottom. Dive depths generally are less than 20 feet and less than 20 seconds long. An able diver, it holds its wings tightly against its body and propels itself with large, webbed feet. Generally feeds during daylight, though may feed at night in areas where there is significant disturbance by humans during the day. In winter, will often form enormous rafts, sometimes containing thousands of ducks. Flight is strong and agile on rapidly beating wings. Able to change direction quickly in mid-air. Frequently forms tight flocks when in flight. Rear-set legs make for awkward walking on land.

CALLS

Usually silent, but female may utter a hoarse *scaup-scaup-scaup* call in flight during winter or when disturbed on the breeding grounds. Male makes soft whistling notes during breeding season.

FOOD

Diet consists of both animal and plant food. In winter, mollusks are a primary food, but it also takes other marine invertebrates such as snails. Also eats fish spawn, as well as sea lettuce and other marine plants. During the breeding season, when it is found in freshwater, a larger proportion of plant food is taken, along with insects and their larvae.

FAMILY LIFE

Monogamous pair. Breeds near bodies of freshwater. Occasionally nests in loose colonies in marshy areas. Female builds the nest on the ground, usually near the water on the shoreline or on a small island. Nest is concealed in dense vegetation and lined with dry plants, grasses and down. The typical clutch of seven to ten eggs is incubated for 23 to 27 days by the female. The precocial young leave the nest soon after hatching and can feed themselves. They are tended by the female for 35 to 42 days. One brood per year.

MIGRATION

Generally arrives on northern breeding grounds during the month of May. Males leave the breeding grounds in late June and form flocks on large lakes, which are often located a significant distance from nesting areas. Fall migration usually occurs between mid-September to late October.

CONSERVATION CONCERNS

Species status overall for North America is secure in the United States and secure in Canada. Because it forms large flocks in coastal environments, the greater scaup is susceptible to oil spills and pollution, especially in the northeastern U.S. where a large percentage of the birds winter. In addition to losing wintering habitat due to urbanization and industrialization, levels of toxins such as PCBs, lead and mercury in birds taken from this region have been high. As a game species it is extremely wary within its wintering range.

Female greater scaup is somewhat drabber than her male counterpart

RELATED SPECIES

The lesser scaup, very similar and almost indistinguishable except on close inspection, belongs to the same genus *Aythya*. The canvasback, redhead and ring-necked duck also belong to this genus.

COMMON EIDER
Somateria mollissima

Male eider shows off its lovely plumage

This beautiful duck, the largest in the Northern Hemisphere, is a year-round resident along the rocky coasts of parts of Alaska and the Arctic, as well as the northeastern United States and Atlantic Canada.

APPEARANCE
Length 24 inches. Wingspan 38 inches. A very large, heavy-bodied duck. Male is a striking black and white. Back, head, neck, throat and breast are white; sides, belly, tail and trailing edge of wings are black. Female is an overall reddish brown. Both sexes have a heavy bill which is gray in winter and yellow in summer.

HABITAT
The most exclusively marine of North American ducks. Found along rocky marine coastlines during both the winter and the breeding

season. Generally found on exposed shorelines, around islands and over shoals and rocky ledges. The female will tend her young in sheltered coves. Often winters as far north as open water exists and in polynyas, large areas of open ocean water surrounded by sea ice.

The range of the common eider

BEHAVIOR

Forages by making deep dives to pick food from the bottom with its powerful bill. Prefers to feed in areas with significant tides, often resting at high tide and feeding during low tide. Brings larger food items to the surface to be prepared for swallowing. Frequently feeds in groups where food is abundant. For example, congregations of eiders occur over large mussel beds in certain passages between islands in the Bay of Fundy. Propels itself underwater using a combination of flapping partially folded wings and powerful paddling with its feet. Will occasionally dabble for food in shallow water. Very strong surface swimmer. Unlike most

A female eider, though less striking than her male counterpart, is beautiful in her own right

DUCKS AND GEESE

sea ducks, its legs are not placed very far to the rear, thus enabling it to be a quite agile and efficient walker. Flight is steady and fast on wings that beat relatively slowly for a duck. Generally stays close to water in flight and often flies in formation in long lines. Can take flight directly from water. Will often form large flocks of more than a thousand birds in winter.

A raft of eiders rests above mussel beds in a tidal passage in the North Atlantic

CALLS

Both sexes may give a low *kor-kor-kor* call when disturbed. Male gives a variety of coos like a rock dove (common pigeon), as well as low moans. Females generally quieter but will utter low raspy quacks.

FOOD

Diet consists mostly of bottom-dwelling invertebrates such as mollusks (particularly mussels) and crustaceans (crabs). Other foods include sea urchins, periwinkles and small fish such as sculpins.

FAMILY LIFE

Monogamous pair. Often nests in colonies. Breeds near coast. Female builds a nest of seaweed, sticks, moss and grass that is lined with large amounts of down. It is usually located in a depression on the ground among rocks or vegetation. The typical clutch of four to five eggs is incubated by the female for 25 to 30 days. Precocial young leave nest soon after hatching. The female toften with the help of another female3assists the young with feeding for 65 to 75 days. One brood per year.

MIGRATION

Some populations in the southern part of the breeding range in eastern North America do not migrate. Other populations usually arrive on breeding grounds between early April and mid-June, depending on the latitude of nesting. Males will leave the breeding grounds in June or July and move to a site where they will molt. Females will do the same in late August and September. Fall migration from the molting areas will generally occur in October and November.

CONSERVATION CONCERNS

Species status overall in North America is secure in the United States and secure in Canada. The common eider is an important species for subsistence hunting in northern regions. It has also come under increasing sport hunting pressure over recent years. Oil and other pollutants also pose a significant threat, especially in parts of its range that lie near shipping lanes, such as those south of Newfoundland where the illegal cleaning of ships' bilges is rampant.

A conservation map for the common eider

RELATED SPECIES

The king and spectacled eiders, two other species found in North America, belong to the same genus *Somateria*.

Did You Know?

While the common eider remains a relatively numerous bird along North America's seacoasts, a close relative, the Labrador duck, is the only North American duck to have become extinct. Although little is known about this somewhat mysterious species, it appears to have relished diving for food over sandbars in the shallow waters near its nesting ground along the southern coast of Labrador and along the Atlantic seaboard of North America where it wintered. Probably never abundant, it was nonetheless heavily hunted along its wintering grounds. The last Labrador duck was shot in 1875 near Long Island, New York.

HARLEQUIN DUCK

Histrionicus histrionicus

One of the most spectacular of all ducks, the male harlequin boasts unmistakable plumage

This beautiful duck is well known for its unusual summer habitat on rushing rivers and streams where it swims with aplomb in and beneath roaring torrents. However, most of its life is spent at sea, near rocky shores where it seems to revel in the crashing winter waves.

APPEARANCE

Length 16.5 inches. Wingspan 26 inches. A small, stocky duck whose name is derived from the ornate costumes of traditional harlequin pantomime actors. Along with the wood duck, it is considered to be one of the most spectacular duck species in North America. Male has a slate blue back, neck, throat, breast, tail and wings with chestnut-colored belly and head accents. Bold, precise white markings on the face, head, neck, breast, wings and base of tail set the male of this species apart from other ducks, even at a distance.

The range of the harlequin duck

Female is overall dull brown with a white spot at the ear and a dull white mask. Both sexes have a relatively long tail, a large rounded head, a small bill and a short neck.

HABITAT

Despite nesting inland near swift rivers and streams, the harlequin spends relatively little time away from the salt water for breeding and males may be absent from coastal areas for only a few weeks of the year. At sea they spend time around rocky islets and shorelines where heavy wave action is the norm; apparently the more rugged the conditions, the better. Usually found very close to shore (often within 100 feet or less) in inter-tidal or sub-tidal areas over rocky ledges or cobble. Often found over kelp and mussel beds. Moves offshore to roost at night.

BEHAVIOR

On salt water the harlequin usually forages by making short dives of 30 seconds or less to shallow depths where it will pick small animals from the bottom. Uses its natural positive buoyancy to carry it back to surface, where it "pops" out of the water like a cork. Will also dabble and pick food items from the surface. Very strong diver. Uses its feet as paddles with wings held out slightly from its body for steering. Extremely strong and agile surface swimmer. Able to contend with crashing surf and rushing water with little difficulty. Will often "scoot" over the water against currents. On inland breeding grounds it will walk upstream along the *bottom* of swift rivers and brooks while picking up aquatic insects and other food items. Quite agile on land compared to other sea duck species, able to hop or walk over rocks and other obstacles. Flight is usually close to the water on rapidly beating wings and can be erratic with sudden direction changes.

CALLS
Usually silent, but still relatively vocal for a sea duck. Most commonly heard call is high-pitched squeak; this has resulted in their being called sea mice in some areas. Also has a variety of less often heard clucking, croaking and scratchy sounds.

FOOD
On salt water (during the non-breeding season), diet consists primarily of bottom-dwelling invertebrates such as crabs, mussels, shrimp, urchins, barnacles and snails. Also takes small bottom fish such as sculpins and rock gunnels. On its breeding grounds it eats mostly aquatic insects and insect larvae.

FAMILY LIFE
Monogamous pair. Breeds on bodies of freshwater. Female builds a ground nest of dried grass, which is lined with down and fine materials, located beneath a bush or among rocks. Usually placed near a stream or river. May also occasionally nest on old tree stumps, on

A raft of male and female harlequin ducks

ledges or in tree cavities in the vicinity of running water. The typical clutch of six to eight eggs is incubated by the female for 27 to 30 days. Although the precocial chicks leave the nest soon after hatching and are able to find their own food, they are tended by the female for 35 or more days. One brood per year.

MIGRATION
Spring arrivals generally reach inland breeding grounds by May. Males and immature females leave the breeding grounds very early, usually arriving at coastal areas in late June or early July. At this point they undergo a molting of their feathers before migrating to other areas where they will spend the fall and winter. Females leave the breeding grounds between July and September, though it's not known where most breeding females molt.

CONSERVATION CONCERNS
Species status overall in North America is apparently secure in the United States and apparently secure in Canada. Though the population is quite healthy in the West, the eastern North American population of the harlequin is listed as a *species of special concern* in Canada. It is listed as endangered in the province of New Brunswick and threatened in the state of Maine. The population in the East is thought to be

between only 1,500 and 2,000 birds. This species is susceptible to oil spills; the Exxon Valdez spill in 1989 is thought to have accounted for the deaths of more than 1,300 birds. Hunting is thought to have contributed to the decline of the eastern population.

A conservation map for the harlequin duck

RELATED SPECIES
The only member of the genus *Histrionicus*.

SURF SCOTER

Melanitta perspicillata

The male surf scoter has a unique, colorful bill

Although it may look unremarkable from a distance, look closely and you will see that this hardy sea duck's face and bizarre, large bill appear to have been designed in a cartoon studio. It is among the least studied of all North American ducks.

APPEARANCE

Length 19 inches. Wingspan 32 inches. Male is black overall with brilliant white patches on the back of the head and the forehead; eye is white. Bill is very large, thick and multicolored in different shades of red, yellow and orange with a large black spot near the base that is surrounded by a large white patch. Female is a dull brown with two faint white patches on the side of its head and a blackish green bill of a similar shape to the male's. No white on wings.

The range of the
surf scoter

HABITAT
Spends most of the year (the non-breeding season) on shallow coastal waters, usually just beyond the surf zone. Found over areas with rocky, cobble or sandy bottoms. During the breeding season they are usually found on clear shallow lakes in the northern interior region of the continent.

BEHAVIOR
Forages by diving to harvest stationary invertebrates that dwell on the bottom. Smaller food items are usually swallowed underwater, while large ones are brought to the surface first. Often seen diving directly in the surf. Propels itself underwater by stroking with its half-folded wings and paddling with its feet, but will also use its feet only. Usually forages in a flock, which will often dive in synchrony. Strong surface swimmer. Flight is rapid and maneuverable on strongly beating wings, and generally low over the water. Must run across water to take off. Less inclined to form flight lines of multiple individuals than other species of scoters. Although it has never been documented scientifically, its rear-set legs likely make movement on land awkward.

CALLS
Usually silent. Male will utter a low gurgling call during courtship and the female gives a raspy *caw* call when young are threatened.

FOOD
In winter, diet consists primarily of marine invertebrates such as mussels and clams, with a smaller proportion of crustaceans. During the breeding season it takes freshwater clams, oysters, aquatic worms, insects, leeches and spiders.

FAMILY LIFE

Monogamous pair. Female builds a bowl-shaped nest lined with down and plant material that is concealed in a clump of vegetation or beneath the bows of an evergreen tree. Located near a lake or pond, and occasionally some distance from water. The typical clutch of five to eight eggs is likely incubated by the female for 28 to 30 days. The precocial young leave the nest soon after hatching and can feed themselves upon reaching the water. The female tends them until they fledge at around 55 days. One brood per year.

MIGRATION

Spring migrants arrive on their breeding grounds in May or June, later in more northerly areas. Fall migration generally occurs between September and November.

CONSERVATION CONCERNS

Species status overall in North America is secure in the United States and secure in Canada. Though still quite numerous, its habit of congregating in large flocks makes the surf scoter extremely vulnerable to oil spills. In this regard, it ranks 14th most vulnerable among 176 species of marine birds in the northeastern Pacific. The situation is similar in the Atlantic.

RELATED SPECIES

Closely related to the white-winged scoter and the black scoter, both of which belong to the genus *Melanitta*.

Male surf scoter

WHITE-WINGED SCOTER

Melanitta fusca

The diagnostic white wing "slash" is visible on this male white-winged scoter

Weighing in at nearly twice the weight of its smaller cousin the surf scoter, this powerful sea duck is the most extensively studied of all the scoter species. Like other scoters it also breeds in Europe and Asia.

APPEARANCE

Length 21 inches. Wingspan 33 inches. A large, husky duck. Males are black overall with a small white wing patch. The red, orange, white and black bill is not as bulky as the surf scoter's. White "comma"-shaped mark behind the eye. The white wing patch is conspicuous in flight. Female is dull brown overall with two indistinct grayish white patches on the head.

HABITAT

Spends fall, winter and early spring along seacoasts of the Atlantic and Pacific. Usually found in shallow bays, estuaries and sounds, also along the open coast and over shoals where shellfish are found. Though it usually remains quite near the shore, it strays into somewhat deeper water than the surf scoter. Some birds overwinter on the Great Lakes. Breeding habitat includes large freshwater and brackish lakes with islands. These are generally located in the western interior of Canada, although the scoter's summer range extends to the Arctic coast of Alaska, the Yukon and the Northwest Territories.

BEHAVIOR

Forages by diving to capture bottom-dwelling invertebrate prey. Picks items (mussels, for example) off bottom, occasionally grasping them in its bill to pull them loose. Dives are generally shallow at less than 20 feet, but occasionally reach depths over 60 feet. An expert diver, it uses partially closed wings in concert with its powerful legs and webbed feet to "fly" underwater. Strong swimmer, able to skitter across water if necessary. Rear-set legs make movement on land awkward, although it will occasionally travel a significant distance from the water to nest. Flight is direct with heavy, rapid wingbeats. Generally flies very low over the water. Must run along the surface while beating its wings to get airborne. Groups often fly in long "strings" over the water. Associates with other scoter species.

CALLS

Usually silent. Occasionally utters a hoarse croak or a low whistle.

FOOD

Diet in winter consists largely of bottom-dwelling invertebrates such as mussels, clams and snails. Sand lance and other small fish are also taken. On its breeding grounds, its diet largely consists of aquatic insects and crustaceans.

FAMILY LIFE

Monogamous pair. Among the latest nesting ducks in North America. Female builds the nest in a hollowed-out area on the ground and lines it with leaves, grasses, twigs and down. Nest is concealed by dense shrubbery. Usually placed on a brushy island in a lake or pond, however nests may be placed a relatively long distance from water. The typical clutch of eight to nine eggs is incubated by the female for 25 to 31 days. Precocial young leave the nest soon after hatching and are quickly able to feed themselves, though they are tended by the female for 63 to 75 days. One brood per year.

The white-winged scoter, a true sea duck

MIGRATION
Birds arrive on their breeding grounds between late April and late May. Fall migration generally occurs between late September and late November. Generally the last of the scoter species to arrive on wintering grounds.

CONSERVATION CONCERNS
Species status overall in North America is secure in the United States and secure in Canada. Although the population appears healthy, this species, like the surf scoter, is highly susceptible to oil spills. Hydroelectric development also poses a risk. Such projects have already had an impact on nesting habitat in Quebec and Labrador.

RELATED SPECIES
Closely related to the surf scoter and the black scoter, which also belong to the genus *Melanitta*. All three scoter species associate on their wintering grounds.

LONG-TAILED DUCK

Clangula hyemalis

Spectacular male long-tailed duck

You will probably hear this duck long before you see it. The most vocal of the sea ducks, its distinctive call can be heard over large distances. Its striking appearance is every bit as unique as its call.

APPEARANCE
Length 21 inches. Wingspan 28 inches. Inland (breeding) and marine (wintering) plumage is very different. Winter males are largely white and black overall with an extremely long, pointed tail. Large dark patch on the side of the head; stubby bill with a heavy flesh-colored band. Female in winter is drab white and brown and lacks the long tail that characterizes the male. In summer, both the male and the female appear much darker overall. The birds are not often seen in this darker plumage, except on breeding grounds in the Arctic.

The range of the
long-tailed duck

HABITAT

The majority of the year is spent on marine coastal waters with a small percentage of the population spending winters on very large, ice-free freshwater bodies of water such as the Great Lakes. Prefers rocky coasts with cobble or rocky bottoms. Most time is spent relatively close to shore, but it may move away from it to feed at productive offshore ledges, shoals and tidal rips. Often roosts well off-shore at night in large congregations. In summer it is found on small freshwater ponds and lakes in the Arctic tundra where it breeds.

BEHAVIOR

Generally forages by diving underwater to pick prey from the bottom or from just above it. Though it generally dives to between 15 and 50 feet, it may be the deepest-diving duck with rare dives to 200 feet. Will also capture prey in mid-water. Very strong diver, using partially folded wings to "fly" underwater. Unlike many other sea ducks, will actively swim to the surface rather than simply relying on its buoyancy to passively ascend. A flock will

A long-tailed duck in flight shows
its characteristic tail feathers

often dive and surface simultaneously. Dives less frequently on summer breeding grounds, relying more on picking prey from the surface of the water. Flight is direct and quick, close to the water, with frequent and erratic side-to-side twists. Walking is awkward due to rather rear-set legs.

CALLS

The male's loud *unk-ow-ow-owdle-ooh* is unmistakable and grows in frequency toward spring, sometimes becoming nearly incessant prior to migration. This call can often be heard a great distance over the water. Both male and female give quiet *chuck-chuck* calls while feeding.

FOOD
Diet consists largely of bottom- or near-bottom-dwelling inverte-brates such as crabs, shrimp, isopods, snails and mussels. Small sand lance, herring, flounder and capelin are among the fish taken. In summer it eats a large proportion of insect larvae.

FAMILY LIFE
Monogamous pair. Female builds a nest of moss, lichens, leaves and other fine vegetation, which is lined with plant material and down. It is located on dry ground (usually on small islands or peninsulas) not far from the water and is well concealed under dwarf willow or other shrubs and grasses. The typical clutch of six or seven eggs is incubated by the female for 24 to 29 days. Precocial young find their own food, but are tended by the female (often with the help of another female) for 35 to 40 days. One brood per year.

CONSERVATION CONCERNS
Species status overall for North America is secure in the United States and secure in Canada. Quite abundant, but vulnerable to oil spills.

RELATED SPECIES
The only member of the genus *Clangula*. Somewhat similar in appearance and habits to the harlequin duck.

A female leads a group of long-tailed ducks in flight

BUFFLEHEAD
Bucephala albeola

A male bufflehead shows its boldly patterned head plumage

A remarkably tough little bird with beautiful plumage, the bufflehead is the smallest of all North American sea ducks.

APPEARANCE
Length 13 inches. Wingspan 21 inches. A very compact species with a large head relative to its body. The male is mostly white overall; head is a dark iridescent green that under most conditions appears to be black. Back of head is covered with a brilliant white patch. The female is dark grayish brown overall; darker on the back and head with a distinctive oval white patch that is located just behind and below the eye. Both sexes have a small bill and a relatively long tail.

HABITAT
Except during the short breeding season, it is generally a coastal

species inhabiting shallow, sandy coves and bays, estuaries and other marine areas that are sheltered from the open sea. Some birds winter on ice-free inland lakes. During the summer it is found in freshwater ponds and lakes, which are located near the mixed coniferous-deciduous woodlands where it builds its nest.

The range of the bufflehead

BEHAVIOR

Forages by diving in shallow water (5 to 13 feet deep) to gather small animals from the bottom. Will also capture fish in mid-water. This efficient underwater swimmer's dives will usually last only a matter of 10 seconds or so. While feeding, all the birds in a group try to dive at the same time, as if each is afraid of being left alone on the surface. Unlike the other diving ducks, the bufflehead sometimes takes flight directly without running along the water, although occasionally short takeoff runs of a few steps can be observed. Is an efficient surface swimmer and is able to get around fairly well on land. Flight is extremely rapid with very quick, almost whirring, wing beats.

CALLS

The male has a squeaky, forced whistle and a rolling, guttural note. Female utters a hoarse *quack*.

FOOD

The diet consists largely of animal food including small fish (especially in saltwater habitats), aquatic insects, amphipods (tiny shrimplike animals) and mollusks. Some seeds are also taken.

FAMILY LIFE

Monogamous pair. The female will line an old woodpecker nest cavity with down and feathers and will occasionally burrow into a natural embankment when tree cavities are scarce. Its small size may have evolved as a result of its habit of nesting in the holes left by northern flicker woodpeckers. The typical clutch of eight to ten eggs is incubated by the female for 28 to 35 days. The precocial young leave the nest after about a day by jumping out of the hole, which is generally between 4 and 20 feet from the ground. The young are tended by female for 50 to 55 days. One brood per year.

MIGRATION
Spring migrants generally arrive on their breeding grounds between early April and early May. Fall migration generally occurs in late October at which time the birds make their way to coastal areas around the continent. Some birds also winter on ice-free lakes.

CONSERVATION CONCERNS
Species status overall in North America is secure in the United States and secure in Canada. The bufflehead may have been much more numerous before widespread hunting in the nineteenth and early twentieth centuries. While still quite common in North America, its numbers appear to be declining in the West. Continued clear-cut logging in the boreal forest has reduced the number of nesting sites available, causing a decline in the overall reproductive success in the species.

RELATED SPECIES
The larger common goldeneye and Barrow's goldeneye ducks are similar in appearance and habits. They also belong in the genus *Bucephala*.

Two females lead this trio of buffleheads in flight

BARROW'S GOLDENEYE

Bucephala islandica

A striking male Barrow's goldeneye

Although it winters along both the Atlantic and Pacific coasts, most of this long-lived sea duck's population breeds in the mountainous regions of British Columbia, the Yukon and Alaska.

APPEARANCE
Length 19 inches. Wingspan 29 inches. Large, puffy-headed duck named for its brilliant yellow eyes. Male appears black and white overall. Black back with conspicuous white spots. Head is black with a purple sheen and a somewhat bulbous forehead. Black tail and stubby bill; white breast and belly. Conspicuous white crescent in front of eye distinguishes this species from the similar common goldeneye, which has an oval white patch. Female has a grayish brown

The range of the
Barrow's
goldeneye

body with a brown head and a yellowish bill that is stubbier than that of the female common goldeneye.

HABITAT

Winters primarily along ice-free seacoasts where it is found in sheltered areas such as inlets, bays and coves; frequents estuaries with rocky shorelines and mussel beds. Brackish water is preferred. Often found in harbors near wharves and other marine installations where mussels grow on pilings. Usually observed quite close to shore. Some birds may winter away from the coast on large ice-free rivers. Breeds on shallow lakes that are located in mountainous areas in the West and high elevation areas in the East. Suitable nesting cavities are required in breeding areas.

BEHAVIOR

Forages by diving to the bottom to capture prey. Dives are usually less than 30 seconds long and less than 20 feet deep. Favors areas with mussel beds. May forage singly, in pairs or in flocks, which often dive synchronously. On breeding grounds it generally favors small, shallow lakes where it dives for invertebrate prey. Swims underwater with its wings held tight against its body while using its webbed feet for propulsion. Strong surface swimmer. Because its legs are located farther forward on its body relative to other sea ducks, it is able to walk fairly well on land. Flight is quite rapid on quickly beating, whistling wings. Usually flies very close to water on shorter flights.

CALLS

Utters low raspy croaks and a catlike mewing sound.

FOOD

While in its saltwater habitat, its diet consists mostly of bottom-dwelling invertebrates such as mussels and periwinkles. Also takes small crabs and other crustaceans, as well as some aquatic plants.

On breeding grounds it feeds on aquatic insects such as caddis fly and dragonfly and their larvae. Also eats some freshwater mollusks and crustaceans as well as aquatic plant seeds.

FAMILY LIFE
Monogamous pair. Female chooses a nest site, which is a cavity in a living or dead tree. Occasionally nests in rock crevices, under brush piles, in a burrow or beneath an old stump. Will also use artificial nesting boxes. Nest is lined with down. Female will often return to the same cavity year after year. Usually located near water but can be over a mile away. The typical clutch of nine or ten eggs is incubated for 28 to 34 days by the female. Precocial young remain in the nest for only 2 to 3 days and can find their own food upon leaving it. Female tends young for 56 days. One brood per year.

MIGRATION
Spring migrants arrive on breeding grounds between late March and mid-May. Fall birds generally arrive on their wintering grounds in November or early December.

CONSERVATION CONCERNS
Species status overall in North America is secure in the United States and secure in Canada. However, the eastern Canadian population has been officially designated as a "species of special concern" due to its small population size. Threats to Barrow's goldeneye include oil spills in wintering areas and logging and development around breeding lakes.

RELATED SPECIES
The bufflehead and the common goldeneye share the same genus *Bucephala*.

Male and female Barrow's goldeneyes

RED-BREASTED MERGANSER

Mergus serrator

A spectacular male red-breasted merganser

With its prominent shaggy crest, thin "saw-tooth" bill and multi-colored plumage, the red-breasted merganser ranks as one of the most distinctive of North America's coastal birds.

APPEARANCE
Length 23 inches. Wingspan 30 inches. A large, but slender sea duck that floats low in the water. Male has a black head with a tinge of iridescent green, a prominent shaggy crest, white ring that almost encircles the throat, dark back, brown breast and white and gray sides. Female has a gray body, a brown neck and a shaggy crest. Both sexes have a long, serrated red bill.

HABITAT
Spends much of the year wintering in coastal marine environments.

Found mostly in protected estuaries, bays and coves, often around harbors and wharves. In eastern North America, also frequents exposed shorelines and rocky headlands. Some red-breasted mergansers winter on the Great Lakes. During breeding season it is found on rivers, lakes, ponds and marshes in the boreal forest zone or tundra regions.

The range of the red-breasted merganser

BEHAVIOR

Forages by making relatively shallow dives to pursue fish underwater, which it snaps up with its "sawtooth" bill. Will often hunt cooperatively in a flock, forming a line prior to diving, and occasionally "beating" the water with the wings to cause fish to school into a shallower depth. While swimming it will dip its specially adapted eyes just below the surface to locate prey. Also searches and probes among rocks underwater to recapture fish that have wiggled loose from its bill. Swims beneath the surface by paddling its webbed feet. Does not use wings when diving. Movement on land is awkward because of rear-set legs. Flight is very strong with very rapid and shallow wing beats. One of the highest sustained flight speeds of any waterfowl with speeds of over 80 miles per hour. Must run and flap along the water to get airborne. Quite wary of humans.

CALLS

Usually silent. Females will occasionally make raspy croaks. During the breeding season males will make a catlike *ee-ow* call.

FOOD

In winter diet consists almost entirely of small fish such as minnows, herring, small sculpins, silversides and killifish. Also known to consume small invertebrates such as shrimp. On its breeding ground it eats several species of salmon parr, sticklebacks, suckers and other small fish species.

FAMILY LIFE

Monogamous pair. Breeds quite late in the season. Female prepares the nest, which is essentially a down-lined, cup-shaped depression in the ground that is concealed beneath low vegetation, or occasionally placed in a low tree stump. Nest is usually located close to freshwater, often on small islands. The typical clutch of eight to ten eggs is incubated for 29 to 35 days by the female. Precocial young leave nest very soon after hatching and are able to find their own food. They are tended by the female for about 60 days. Broods of separate breeding pairs will often be combined and looked after by multiple females. One brood per year.

MIGRATION

One of the later waterfowl migrants. Most birds arrive on their breeding grounds from mid- to late May. Fall migration is quite prolonged and generally begins in late August before peaking in late November.

CONSERVATION CONCERNS

Species status overall in North America is secure in the United Sates and secure in Canada. Although its population numbers about 250,000 birds, the great majority are western breeders with fewer than 10 percent in the East. The red-breasted merganser's wintering habitat is vulnerable to oil spills.

RELATED SPECIES

Its larger cousin, the common merganser, belongs to the same genus *Mergus*. The smaller hooded merganser is in a separate genus.

The female red-breasted merganser lacks the male's bold plumage

SHOREBIRDS

WILSON'S PLOVER

Charadrius wilsonia

A Wilson's plover on a white sand beach; its long legs and heavy bill are evident

One of the most exclusively coastal of all the members of the plover family, this inconspicuous little shorebird is rarely found far from the seashore.

APPEARANCE
Length 8 inches. Wingspan 19 inches. Somewhat larger than its sibling species, the piping, snowy and semi-palmated plovers, it has dark brown upperparts, a blackish neck band and white underparts. The head, which appears a little large for the bird's body, has a dark crown. The heavy black bill is larger than those of other small species of plovers. Large black eyes. Flesh-tone legs are somewhat longer than other small plovers.

The range of the
Wilson's plover

HABITAT

Sandy and pebble beaches, sandbars, tidal mudflats and pools, storm-washed points, the edges of lagoons, near river mouths and inlets. Doesn't normally stray far from the coast.

BEHAVIOR

Often associates with the terns and oystercatchers that share its habitat. Forages much like other small plovers by walking or running along the beach or mudflat while picking prey from the surface. Also probes in the mud, sand or shallow water. Will often run along the beach to flee danger rather than taking flight. Flight is rapid and direct on quickly beating wings. Female will draw intruders away from its nest by performing a distraction display where she feigns injury.

CALLS

An abrupt whistled *weet* or a double whistled phrase.

FOOD

Small crabs, other crustaceans, sand worms, insects, small mollusks, marine worms, various aquatic larvae and eggs of marine invertebrates.

FAMILY LIFE

Monogamous pair. Nests in loose colonies, occasionally in the proximity of terns and oystercatchers. The male scrapes a shallow depression in sand or gravel above the tide line amid concealing shells, pebbles, plant stems or driftwood. Usually placed near an object such as a tuft of grass. The clutch of two to four eggs is incubated for 23 to 24 days by both sexes. Young are fed by both parents for 21 days. One brood per year.

A Wilson's plover rests in the sand in the heat of the mid-day sun

MIGRATION
Less migratory than other small North American plovers. Birds in the northern part of the breeding range migrate to the coastal southern United States during the winter. Most southern birds are resident year-round.

CONSERVATION CONCERNS
Overall species status in North America is apparently secure in the United States. A population of only 6,000 birds in the United States is a cause for concern. This species often nests along shoreline that is suitable for human development, and this may threaten the bird's survival in the future.

RELATED SPECIES
One of six plovers in the genus *Charadrius* that regularly breed in North America.

AMERICAN OYSTERCATCHER

Haematopus palliatus

An American oystercatcher with freshly caught prey in its bill

This striking shorebird, with its clownish appearance, large blood-red bill and chunky size stands out boldly from the rather drab plovers and sandpipers associating with it on coasts around the United States.

APPEARANCE
Length 17 inches. Wingspan 32 inches. A large, heavy-bodied shorebird, with a black head and neck, dark brown back and white underparts. Distinctive bright red, long and laterally compressed bill. Yellow eye with bright red eye-ring; pale legs. Bold white wing stripe conspicuous in flight.

HABITAT
Includes coastal beaches, mudflats, lagoons, rocky shorelines, islands and other saltwater wetlands. Seldom found inland.

BEHAVIOR

Forages by probing in the mud or sand then extracting clams, oysters and other shellfish. Also picks food from the surface and from shallow water. It inserts its bill (which is triangular in cross-section making it very rigid) into the bivalve to partly open the shell, then severs the adductor muscle holding the two halves together. Usually solitary or in small groups. Very agile on the ground, and quite an efficient walker/runner. Flight is rapid and steady on quickly beating wings.

The range of the American oystercatcher

CALLS

Gives an insistent, piercing *wheep wheep wheep* call when disturbed. A loud *krik krik krik* is given when taking flight.

FOOD

Diet includes bivalves such as oysters, clams and mussels. Also takes crabs, marine worms, urchins and occasionally fish.

American oystercatchers capture small animals such as shellfish and worms by probing their long bills into the sand or mud

FAMILY LIFE

Monogamous pair. Solitary breeder; occasionally nests in loose colonies. Both sexes build the nest, which is merely a shallow depression in the sand or gravel, with a few bits of shell as a lining. Nest usually located on a relatively elevated area on an upper part of the beach. Often located amid clumps of vegetation, pebbles and broken shells. The typical clutch of two eggs is incubated by both adults for 24 to 29 days. Precocial young leave nest shortly after hatching and are tended by both parents for 35 or more days. One brood per year.

MIGRATION

Generally a year-round resident throughout most of its range. Birds breeding in more northerly areas migrate.

CONSERVATION CONCERNS

Species status overall in North America is secure in the United States. Population estimated to be approximately 9,000. Oystercatchers were nearly brought to extinction due to hunting in the late nineteenth and early twentieth centuries, resulting in a range contraction away from former breeding areas in the Northeast. In the 1800s, Audubon reported that they bred as far north as Labrador. Happily, it appears the population is growing slowly and expanding northward once again, reaching Massachusetts.

The "knife-edge" shape of the American oystercatcher's specialized bill is visible here

RELATED SPECIES

The black oystercatcher belongs to the same genus, *Haematopus*.

BLACK OYSTERCATCHER

Haematopus bachmani

A black oystercatcher

This large, distinctive shorebird, a West Coast specialist, is not likely to be mistaken for any other species along rocky Pacific coasts.

APPEARANCE
Length 17 inches. Wingspan 32 inches. A crow-sized shorebird with completely black or blackish brown plumage. Unlike many shorebirds, the black oystercatcher shows no white on its wings when in flight. Long, straight, red bill; yellow eye with orange eye-ring. Stout pinkish legs and feet.

HABITAT
Found exclusively along Pacific shorelines. Usually inhabits exposed rocky coasts with heavy surf, but also frequents sheltered rocky bays and inlets in winter. Will also feed on mudflats.

Breeding areas may also include gravel and sandy beaches, often located on islands. Avoids forested islands for breeding sites.

BEHAVIOR

Forages largely in the rocky inter-tidal and surf zone. Often "jumps" out of the way of crashing waves. Once it locates a mussel or other bivalve shellfish, it pecks a small hole in the shell then uses its specialized bill to cut the adductor muscle that holds the shell halves together. Will search for and pry limpets from the surfaces of rocks. Also probes for clams in the mud and sand. Will occasionally hunt for small crabs on sandy beaches. Walks efficiently with fairly long strides. Flight is direct and rapid on shallowly beating wings.

The range of the black oystercatcher

CALLS

Call is a loud, clear whistle-like *queep*.

FOOD

Diet includes sea, bay and horse mussels, limpets, sea urchins, marine worms, crabs, barnacles and clams. Also takes herring eggs when available.

FAMILY LIFE

Monogamous pair. Both sexes participate in building the nest, which is a depression in a grassy, sandy or pebbly area above the high tide mark. It is lined with bits of shells or small pebbles. The typical clutch of two eggs is incubated by both adults for 24 to 36 days. The precocial young leave the nest soon after hatching and are tended by both parents for 30 to 35 days. One brood per year.

MIGRATION

Habits not well known. Generally non-migratory throughout most of its range, although it is thought that northern populations may migrate.

CONSERVATION CONCERNS
Species status overall in North America is secure in the United States and apparently secure in Canada. Overall population is small, perhaps fewer than 10,000. Species has been extirpated in several areas in Alaska because of the introduction of red and Arctic foxes on breeding islands. Also susceptible to oil spills. Twenty percent of the population inhabiting Prince William Sound in Alaska was killed by the Exxon Valdez oil spill in 1989.

RELATED SPECIES
This and the American oystercatcher are the only species of oyster-catcher in North America. Both belong to the genus *Haematopus*.

Black oystercatchers spend much of their time on rocky areas of the shore

WHIMBREL

Numenius phaeopus

The long, curved bill of the whimbrel is a specialized tool for probing for food

A very large shorebird with an unmistakable bill, the long-lived whimbrel is the widest-ranging and most coastal member of the curlew family in North America.

APPEARANCE
Length 17.5 inches. Wingspan 32 inches. Overall speckled brown plumage with bold dark head stripes. The bill is extremely long and thin with an obvious downward curve. Legs are long and gray. Wings are relatively long and pointed.

HABITAT
During winter it is found primarily along the coast on tidal mud-flats. Also found in estuaries, lagoons, salt marshes, along sand beaches and occasionally on rocky shorelines. Also found inland on

lakes and rivers. During migration will visit coastal barrens and heaths with crowberry, bilberry, cloudberries and blueberries and other low plants. Breeds in Arctic habitats including tundra, bogs, taiga and uplands.

The range of the whimbrel

BEHAVIOR

Forages by probing into mud to find small prey such as worms and other invertebrates. Interestingly, the curve of the bill closely matches the curve of the fiddler crab's burrow, a major winter prey species. Will break bits off fiddler crabs and other larger prey before swallowing. Also lunges at surface prey. Will capture insects and pick berries with the tip of the bill. Very efficient at walking and running on land. Like other shorebirds, it will occasionally rest on one leg with the other tucked against the body. Flight is direct with moderate, steady wing beats and an extended neck and legs. Often seen flying in a "V" or in long straight lines during migration.

CALLS

Most commonly heard is the flight call, a single note repetitive series of whistled *pip-pip-pip-pip-pip*. Also performs a series of musical notes on the breeding grounds.

FOOD

Diet varies depending on time of year. During migration and winter when most whimbrels are found along seacoasts, they eat a wide variety of small crabs and other crustaceans, marine worms, bivalve shellfish, small fish and insects. On the breeding grounds insects are the food of choice. Berries are also taken when animal food is in short supply.

FAMILY LIFE

Monogamous pair; long-term pair bond. Will occasionally nest in loose colonies. Both sexes (primarily the female) build a shallow nest lightly lined with moss, grass and lichens. It is located in a small clump of grass or on the ground in an open area of the tundra. The typical clutch of four eggs is incubated by both adults for 22 to 28 days. The precocial young leave the nest and can feed themselves soon after hatching, but are tended by both parents for 35 to 40 days. One brood per year.

A pair of whimbrels displaying their wings

MIGRATION

A long-distance migrant. Some birds travel between their high Arctic breeding grounds and the southern tip of South America. Like many other shorebirds, whimbrels will move to coastal areas in Canada and the United States after the breeding season to "fatten up" prior to the long migration to southern wintering areas. Spring migrants generally arrive on their breeding grounds in May and June. Fall migration to North American coasts usually occurs in July and August, with birds departing these areas for South America after that.

CONSERVATION CONCERNS

Species status overall in North America is secure in the United States and secure in Canada. Though hunted extensively in the 1800s for food, the population has rebounded since the enactment of the U.S.-Canada Migratory Birds Convention in 1916. The destruction of wintering habitats in South America may pose a threat to the whimbrel.

RELATED SPECIES

One of three species of curlews breeding in North America. The other two are the long-billed curlew and the bristle-thighed curlew. All belong to the genus *Numenius*. Another species, the Eskimo curlew, is probably extinct.

RUDDY TURNSTONE
Arenaria interpres

A ruddy turnstone in winter plumage

This somewhat pugnacious little shorebird is unmistakable for its boldly patterned plumage and its relative tameness.

APPEARANCE
Length 9.5 inches. Wingspan 17 inches. A small shorebird with variegated plumage. Back and wings are mottled reddish brown, black and white (duller during non-breeding season when they are most commonly seen). Black "bib" on breast, black and white face, white chin patch. Black bill is medium length, chisel-shaped and somewhat upturned at the end. Underparts are white. Neck is short. Orange legs are short and a little stocky.

HABITAT
In fall, spring and winter it inhabits rocky coastlines, sand and gravel

beaches, mudflats and estuaries, particularly where there is an abundance of seaweed and other debris washed ashore. Sometimes visits inland wetlands, lakes and other freshwater bodies during migration. During the brief summer breeding season it is found along rocky coasts, marshy shores, wet lowlands and tundra of the Arctic.

The range of the ruddy turnstone

BEHAVIOR

A highly opportunistic bird that employs several feeding techniques. Is named for its unique foraging behavior that involves working its way along the shoreline flipping stones, shells and other items as it searches for food. Capable of moving surprisingly large objects using this technique. Also digs and probes in the sand and pecks and stabs with its sharp bill. Pries open shellfish and is able to tear strips of flesh from carrion. Known to occasionally enter gull and tern colonies to break open and eat the contents of unattended eggs. Able to run very quickly and efficiently in pursuit of prey on the ground. Flight is swift and direct on quickly beating wings. Tends to be tame.

Ruddy turnstones are named for their habit of "turning" stones and other items on the beach as they look for food

CALLS
Call is a low, harsh *ket-i-ket*. Alarm call is a simple *kek*.

FOOD
During the non-breeding season diet includes primarily invertebrates including mollusks, crustaceans, worms, brittle stars, sea urchins and snails. Eats mostly insects during the breeding season, as well as some small fish, and occasionally the eggs of other species of birds.

FAMILY LIFE
Monogamous pair. The female builds a nest, which is a depression in the ground lined with dried bits of plants, seaweed or moss.

Ruddy turnstone resting on one leg, a common practice of shorebirds

Usually placed on the Arctic tundra not far from water and often near a gull or tern colony. The typical clutch of four eggs is incubated by both sexes for 21 to 24 days. The precocial young can feed themselves soon after hatching but are tended by both adults for 19 to 21 days. One brood per year.

MIGRATION
A long-distance migrant that usually arrives on its spring breeding grounds from late May to early June. Fall departure from the breeding grounds generally occurs between late July and early September.

CONSERVATION CONCERNS
Species status overall for North America is secure in the United States and secure in Canada. Though still quite common, this species, like many other shorebirds, is vulnerable to disturbance, pollution and habitat destruction of its migratory feeding areas and wintering grounds.

RELATED SPECIES
One of two species in North America belonging to the genus *Arenaria*. The other is the black turnstone.

SANDERLING
Calidris alba

A sanderling showing the remnants of its reddish brown breeding plumage

This species' name speaks volumes about its life history: it is the most sandy beach loving of all the shorebirds, and is only occasionally found in other habitats.

APPEARANCE
Length 8 inches. Wingspan 15 inches. A small but chunky bird, lighter in color overall than any other similar-sized shorebird, especially during the non-breeding season. In winter (when most people will see it) it is mostly white overall with a gray back, black legs and a black bill. In the breeding season its back and wings are reddish brown. A conspicuous white wing stripe is visible when the bird is in flight.

HABITAT

Prefers sandy beaches almost exclusively, especially hard-packed ones. Can occasionally be found on tidal sandflats and mudflats and rocky shores. Sometimes found inland along the sandy or muddy margins of ponds, rivers and lakes, rarely far from the ocean. Breeding habitat is generally on coastal tundra, islands and peninsulas located above the Arctic Circle.

The range of the sanderling

BEHAVIOR

Foraging technique is familiar to many people who have visited temperate beaches in the winter. Almost always feeds in the wet interwave or intertidal zone of the beach. Runs very quickly along the water line picking and probing for small invertebrates. Will run rapidly as it is "chased" up the beach by incoming waves only to run back down again to pick up the tiny animals that have been left high and dry by the receding wave. Often feeds in flocks. Also runs through shallow pools and puddles while using its bill to skim the surface of the water for food. Occasionally will feed on the upper beach among dead seaweed and other debris washed ashore. Extremely fast runner. Flight is very strong and rapid on quickly beating wings. Forms tightly packed flocks on the wing and often flies low in the vicinity of the feeding area.

CALLS

Most often heard sound is a shrill *quick-quick* that is given when the birds are flushed from the beach. Also utters a loud *cree* call.

FOOD

During the non-breeding season its diet consists mainly of invertebrates such as tiny crabs, amphipods, isopods and mollusks. On breeding grounds will take insects and insect larvae, as well as plant matter when animal food isn't available.

FAMILY LIFE

Monogamous pair. Occasionally polyandrous (female mating with more than one male). Nests in pairs or sometimes in loose colonies. Both sexes participate in building the nest, which is a cup-shaped depression lined with dried bits of plants, moss and lichens, located in a high, dry, rocky part of the tundra. The typical clutch of three to four eggs is incubated mostly by the male for 24 to 31 days (females will often have one mate incubate the eggs while she finds another male to have a second brood with). Precocial young leave the nest and can feed themselves soon after hatching, but are tended by at least one parent for 17 days. One or two broods per year.

MIGRATION

Spring migrants usually arrive on their breeding grounds in late May or early June. Fall migration generally begins in late July. Likely the most widely distributed wintering shorebird in the Americas, it is found from 50° north in British Columbia to 50° south near the southern tip of South America.

In winter, sanderlings are much less colorful than in summer

A sanderling forages along a beach

CONSERVATION CONCERNS
Species status overall in North America is apparently secure in the United States and secure in Canada. Vulnerable to development and oil spills along the coasts where it spends its winters. Global warming may have an impact on its high Arctic nesting habitat as it causes changes in the northern ecosystem.

RELATED SPECIES
One of nine species in North America that belong to the genus *Calidris*. There are forty-three species in the Family *Scolopacidae* in North America.

DUNLIN

Calidris alpina

A winter-plumage dunlin rests on one leg

One of the widest-ranging of all shorebirds, the dunlin breeds throughout the Northern Hemisphere and spends its winters in large flocks along the southern seacoasts of the continent.

APPEARANCE
Length 8.5 inches. Wingspan 17 inches. A medium-sized sandpiper. Species has two seasonal plumages. Winter plumage (when the bird is most likely to be observed in temperate areas) is an overall dull gray brown. Birds in breeding plumage, which may be observed as they migrate north in the spring, are much more distinctive with a rufous red back, pale head and a black belly. Legs are black. Bill is quite long, thin and droops toward the end.

HABITAT

In winter and during migration it is found on coastal estuaries, beaches, mudflats, sandflats, lagoons, salt marsh wetlands and also on inland wetlands. During its breeding season it inhabits wet and boggy Arctic tundra areas with plenty of water, coastal sedge meadows and sedge marshes.

The range of the dunlin

BEHAVIOR

Forages like a typical sandpiper by wading in shallow water along shores and on mud and sand flats while probing and jabbing its bill into the ground to capture prey items. As it feeds it thrusts its bill rapidly up and down into the mud. Often probes with an open bill to taste prey. Will also jab and peck at prey on the surface. Usually feeds in flocks, some very large. Like other shorebirds, it is very efficient at moving about on land and will often sleep while standing on one leg. Flight is very fast on rapidly beating wings. On one occasion a dunlin was clocked flying at over 100 miles per hour.

CALLS

Flight call is a raspy *creeps*.

FOOD

Diet includes invertebrates such as worms, mud shrimp, small crustaceans and bivalves, as well as insects and their larvae.

FAMILY LIFE

Monogamous pair. More than one nest location may be prepared by both sexes, but the final site is chosen by the female. The nest is a shallow scrape on the ground that is lined with grasses and other bits of vegetation. The typical clutch of four eggs is incubated by both sexes for 20 to 23 days. The precocial young leave the nest soon after hatching and can feed themselves right away, but are tended by both parents (mostly the male) for 19 to 21 days. One brood per year, occasionally two.

MIGRATION
Migrates a shorter distance than many of the smaller sandpipers, traveling from the Arctic to the east and west coasts of Canada and the United States. Spring migrants generally arrive on their breeding grounds between mid-May and mid-June. Fall migration occurs between late July and late October.

CONSERVATION CONCERNS
Species status overall in North America is secure in the United States and secure in Canada. Despite a large population of over a half million birds, populations have declined in recent years. Loss of wintering and migration staging habitats poses a threat to the species.

RELATED SPECIES
Three sub-species of dunlins exist in North America: the western, the interior and the eastern race. One of nine species in North America that belong to the genus *Calidris*.

A dunlin in its reddish breeding plumage

GULLS, TERNS
AND SKIMMERS

PARASITIC JAEGER

Stercorarius parasiticus

Parasitic jaegers are powerful, highly agile fliers

This graceful member of the gull family, known as a skua in Europe, is one of the archetypal pirates of the bird world. It steals fish from terns and gulls by relentlessly harassing them until they drop their prey.

APPEARANCE

Length 16.5 inches. Wingspan 46 inches. Somewhat falcon-like in appearance. Overall, dark back and wings with white underparts. Light area often visible on the undersides of the wings. Breast, throat, neck and cheeks are a creamy white. Dark cap on the head. Relatively small, thin bill. Long pointed tail feathers. A small percentage of dark color morph birds are charcoal gray.

HABITAT

The range of the parasitic jaeger

In winter it is a seabird through and through. Found offshore along the southern Atlantic seaboard, the Gulf of Mexico and California coasts of the U.S. where it often travels among flocks of terns and gulls. Occasionally can be observed from shore. Spends more time close to shore than the other jaeger species. During migration it is found along the coasts of North America from Florida and California to the Arctic. Its Arctic breeding habitat is on flat grassy areas of the tundra or on stony ground near the coast.

BEHAVIOR

Aggressive, opportunistic feeder. Chases terns and gulls in flight, causing them to drop their prey which is then grabbed in mid-air by the jaeger. With amazing falcon-like agility, it will occasionally capture small birds on the wing. During the breeding season it preys on ground-nesting birds and their eggs, as well as capturing small mammals. Often swallows prey whole, fur (or feathers) and all. Scavenges when possible. Will follow humans and other mammals as they visit bird nesting colonies and swoop down behind them to grab eggs or chicks from nests that the nesting adults have just been frightened off. Rarely visits land outside of the breeding season. Swims like a gull. Very swift flight on quick, shallow wing beats.

CALLS

Mostly silent, except on its breeding grounds where it yelps and squeals. Also utters a rising mewing sound.

FOOD

Wide-ranging diet includes fish and marine invertebrates pirated from other seabirds. Feeds on the eggs and young of ground-nesting birds such as eiders, shorebirds, ptarmigan and terns. Also eats lemmings and other small mammals. Scavenges detritus and carcasses on beaches and will eat berries.

FAMILY LIFE
Monogamous pair; long-term bond. Often nests in colonies. Both sexes (mostly female) build a nest in a shallow depression in the grass or moss (often on a hummock) that is lightly lined with plant material. Usually located on a slope or at the base of a cliff. The typical clutch of two eggs is incubated by both adults for 25 to 28 days. The semi-precocial young are fed by both parents for 21 days. One brood per year.

MIGRATION
Travels from breeding areas throughout the Arctic to become a true seabird species during migration and winter when it spends all its time on the ocean, rarely if ever coming to land. May migrate as far as southern South America. Spring migrants generally arrive on their breeding grounds from early May to mid-June. Fall migration generally occurs between late August and October.

CONSERVATION CONCERNS
Species status overall in North America is secure in the United States and secure in Canada.

RELATED SPECIES
A member of the large gull family Laridae and one of five members of the genus *Stercorarius*, which also includes the long-tailed and pomarine jaegers, and the great and south polar skuas.

Did You Know?
Thousands of modern-day pirates ply the seas and skies around North America. Not the Blackbeard kind, but those with wings and beaks. Species such as the parasitic jaeger, the magnificent frigatebird and the great black-backed gull have used intimidation and

harassment as their stock-in-trade for thousands of years. "Thou shalt not steal" means nothing to such species. They routinely attack usually smaller birds in mid-air to force them to drop their prey, which is then snapped up by the aggressor before it hits the water. A frigatebird chasing a white pelican through the air (both of them are enormous birds) as they twist this way and that until the pelican drops its fish is a sight not soon forgotten.

LAUGHING GULL

Larus atricilla

A laughing gull in breeding plumage

This attractive, medium-sized gull, named for its unusual call, is a common sight along much of North America's Atlantic coast.

APPEARANCE
Length 17 inches. Wingspan 40 inches. In summer it sports a black hood that distinguishes it from any other gull on the coast at that time of year. Slate gray back and wings with white belly and underparts. Wings darken toward the ends and have black tips. Small white crescents directly above and below the eye. Relatively long, pointed, dark red bill droops slightly toward the end. Black legs. In winter the black hood is replaced by indistinct dark smudges on the head and the bill becomes almost black.

HABITAT

Found on or not far from the coast in all seasons. Frequents beaches, estuaries, bays, lagoons, river mouths and salt marshes. Will often roost a short distance inland on lakes, marshes and water impoundments. Often seen in the vicinity of fishing piers. Nesting habitat includes salt marshes, rocky islands with vegetation, sand beaches and islands, and sand spits.

The range of the laughing gull

BEHAVIOR

Forages in typical gull fashion by walking along the shore, the mudflats or in shallow water while picking up food items from the surface or just below it. Also feeds while swimming on the surface and dipping its bill underwater to catch prey. Occasionally plunge dives for fish. Seizes insects while in flight. Often steals fish from terns and will opportunistically hang around pelicans to catch any prey that has escaped them. Less of a scavenger than most gulls, although it will feed at garbage dumps at times. A relatively efficient walker that is quite agile in its pursuit of food on the ground. Flight is buoyant and relatively slow on deep wing beats. Often soars on thermals and updrafts.

A laughing gull "laughs" in its drab winter plumage

CALLS

A very vocal bird. Commonly heard flight call is a clear *ha-ha-ha*. Also performs a repetitive *kak-kak-kak-kak-kak* alarm call, among others.

FOOD

An opportunistic feeder with a wide array of food in its diet. Takes fish, aquatic invertebrates such as squid, worms, crabs and shrimp, as well as insects, berries, offal and human garbage.

FAMILY LIFE

Monogamous pair. Breeds in colonies. Both sexes build a shallow scrape nest woven from coarse grass that is lightly lined with grass, twigs and other debris and placed in tall grass, under bushes or in other concealing vegetation. The typical clutch of three eggs is incubated by both adults for 20 days. The semi-precocial young leave the nest a few days after hatching and are fed by both parents for 35 days. One brood per year.

MIGRATION

Southern breeding birds generally do not migrate. In other areas, spring migrants generally arrive on their breeding grounds by mid-May. Fall migration usually starts in late August with the bulk of birds migrating in October.

CONSERVATION CONCERNS

Species status overall in North America is secure in the United States and critically imperiled in Canada as a breeding bird since it only *formerly* bred there.

RELATED SPECIES

One of thirteen gull species belonging to the genus *Larus* that breed in North America.

A conservation status map for the laughing gull

BLACK-HEADED GULL

Larus ridibundus

In winter, the black-headed gull can be easily distinguished from the similar Bonaparte's gull by its reddish orange legs and bill

In North America this species breeds in small numbers in a few isolated spots in Newfoundland. However, it is a regular to rare winter visitor elsewhere in Atlantic Canada and the northeastern U.S. In Europe, it is one of the most abundant gulls.

APPEARANCE

Length 16 inches. Wingspan 40 inches. Similar in appearance to the Bonaparte's gull. In winter it has a light gray back and wings (lighter than the Bonaparte's) with dark wing tips. The rest of the bird is white except for varying amounts of light gray on the head and dark smudges near the ear and in front of the eye. During the breeding season it has a dark brown head. Bill, legs and feet are reddish at all times of year.

HABITAT

In winter it inhabits the low-lying shores and waters along the Atlantic coast (infrequently south of Atlantic Canada) where it may be found on beaches, coves, lagoons, inlets, estuaries, tidal flats, bays, salt marshes and in fishing harbors. In Europe it has become very well adapted to human-populated areas along the coast. Doesn't normally stray far from land. Breeds on coastal islands, dunes, salt marshes and freshwater lakes and rivers.

The range of the black-headed gull

BEHAVIOR

Feeds on a wide variety of food types. Forages by dipping its bill beneath the water for prey, as well as seizing prey directly at the surface while it swims. Like the Bonaparte's gull, it will swoop down on the wing, patter its feet on the surface without landing and grab food from the water. Occasionally does shallow plunge dives into the water. Pecks at food in seaweed, and pulls worms from the sand or mud. Hawks for insects. Often pirates food from smaller birds. Will occasionally eat human garbage. Swims like a typical gull. Quite an efficient and agile walker. Flight is buoyant on long, slender wings.

CALLS

Calls are varied but the most commonly heard are a harsh, crow-like *kwaar* or a yelping *keer*. Calls are somewhat lower than those of the Bonaparte's gull.

FOOD

Will eat almost anything it can handle. Diet includes fish, clams, urchins, crustaceans, marine worms, earthworms, insects, berries, seeds, carrion and garbage.

FAMILY LIFE

Monogamous pair. Breeds in colonies. Both sexes build a moss-and-grass-lined nest of plant matter on the ground. Usually located in a marsh or other open area. Will often steal nesting material from unguarded nearby nests. The typical clutch of three eggs is incubated for 23 to 26 days by both adults. During the approximately 10 days that the semi-precocial young remain in the nest, they are fed by both parents. One brood per year.

MIGRATION

Most birds seen in North America are wintering birds that likely breed in Iceland, the Faroe Islands and other parts of northern Europe. The few birds that breed in Newfoundland are probably year-round residents and do not migrate any great distance.

CONSERVATION STATUS

Species status overall in North America is vulnerable in the United States and vulnerable in Canada due to the relatively small wintering populations.

In summer, the black-headed gull's head is actually dark brown

RELATED SPECIES

A member of the large gull genus *Larus*. Most similar species is the Bonaparte's gull.

BONAPARTE'S GULL

Larus philadelphia

An adult winter-plumage Bonaparte's gull in flight

Named for Napoleon's nephew, zoologist Charles Lucien, few birds can match the aerial abilities of the little Bonaparte's gull. With light, effortless wing beats, it bounds buoyantly through the strongest coastal winds with grace and apparent ease.

APPEARANCE
Length 13 inches. Wingspan 34 inches. One of our smallest gulls. Roughly the size of a tern. On its coastal winter range it is overall white with a light gray back. Head is white with a dark spot behind the eye; bill is small and black. Wings are gray with the trailing edge of the tips black and the leading edge showing a white triangle. Rest of body white. In summer, the Bonaparte's has a black hood and white eye-ring.

HABITAT

Winters along the east and west coasts of North America, as well as the Gulf of Mexico. Prefers sheltered bays, harbors, mudflats and beaches. Feeds farther offshore than most gull species, often found up to 12 miles from the coast. Favors areas with tides or currents. Some populations winter on lakes, ponds and wetlands. During spring migration it is often found feeding on spawning herring along the Pacific coast. During the breeding season it is found in northern wetlands, in the vicinity of lakes and ponds, and near the edge of the boreal forest.

The range of the Bonaparte's gull

BEHAVIOR

One of the most diverse foraging repertoires of any gull. Flies close to the water and "dips" to grab food from the surface, or does very shallow plunge dives into the water to capture small fish and other prey. Also picks food from the water while swimming on the surface, as well as seizing prey while wading. Forages on land, running very quickly in pursuit of tiny invertebrates on the beach. Flight is very light on quickly beating wings. A highly maneuverable flier. Able to hover and soar efficiently. Is an agile swimmer while pursuing prey, often swimming rapidly in little circles to pick insects off the water. Walks with a typical gull waddle.

CALLS

Most commonly heard call is a harsh *cheer cheer.*

FOOD

Opportunistic feeder, eating whatever suitably sized items are available. Small fish, fish eggs, snails, marine worms, crustaceans and other marine prey are taken. During breeding season it eats mainly insects.

FAMILY LIFE

Monogamous pair. Both sexes build a cup-shaped nest of sticks, moss and other plant matter from 4 to 20 feet up in a coniferous tree, which is usually located near a lake or a pond. The typical clutch of three eggs is incubated for 24 days by both sexes. The semi-precocial young are fed by both parents while they remain in the nest. One brood per year.

MIGRATION
Spring migrants arrive on breeding grounds between late April and late May. Fall migration generally occurs between mid-July and early September.

CONSERVATION CONCERNS
Species status overall in North America is secure in the United States and secure in Canada.

RELATED SPECIES
One of thirteen breeding North American gulls belonging to the genus *Larus*. Similar in appearance to the black-headed gull.

A first-year Bonaparte's gull in flight

RING-BILLED GULL

Larus delawarensis

The dark "ring" on its bill is a distinctive characteristic of the ring-billed gull

An extremely widespread and abundant gull, the ring-billed can be found during the non-breeding season along nearly every coastal area of the United States as well as more southerly Canadian coasts.

APPEARANCE
Length 17 inches. Wingspan 48 inches. A medium-sized gull with a white head and underparts, a pale gray back, relatively short, bright yellow bill with a distinctive black ring, and yellow legs. Black wing tips are conspicuous during flight. Young birds don't attain full adult plumage until their third year.

HABITAT
Generally found near the coast and around offshore islands during the non-breeding season. Generally breeds (and often winters)

inland on freshwater lakes, ponds, marshes and rivers, and is quite common around the Great Lakes.

The range of the ring-billed gull

BEHAVIOR

A generalist forager that will take advantage of most feeding opportunities. Captures insects on the wing. Like a shorebird, feeds along the water's edge on beaches, where it captures crustaceans, mollusks and other invertebrates as well as fish. Follows fishing boats and lingers around fish processing plants for offal. Frequents garbage dumps and freshly plowed agricultural fields. Often pirates food from species such as cormorants, as well as from the terns and smaller gulls with which it sometimes associates. Flight is powerful and quite buoyant on slow-beating wings. Spends much of its time on the water, but like most gull species it is not a particularly efficient swimmer.

CALLS

Typical gull cries. Calls are scratchy and somewhat softer and higher pitched than the herring gull's.

FOOD

Diet includes fish, insects, worms, crustaceans, mollusks and other marine invertebrates, as well as fish offal and garbage.

FAMILY LIFE

Monogamous pair. Occasionally polygynous. Nests in ground colonies, often with other species of gulls and terns. Both sexes participate in building the flat nest of weeds, grass and sometimes trash on an elevated spot on open ground (sometimes concealed by vegetation), usually located on an island. The typical clutch of two to four eggs is incubated by both adults for 21 days. The semi-precocial young are tended and fed by both parents for 35 days. One brood annually.

MIGRATION
Migratory over most of its range but it will overwinter in many places. Spring migrants usually arrive on their breeding grounds from late March to early May. Fall migration generally occurs between September and November.

CONSERVATION CONCERNS
Overall status in North America is secure in the United States and secure in Canada. Worldwide population estimated in the millions and growing.

RELATED SPECIES
One of thirteen gulls belonging to the genus *Larus* that regularly breed in North America.

A ring-billed gull pecking at a dead fish

HERRING GULL

Larus argentatus

Although extremely abundant and approaching the status of pest in many places, the herring gull is nevertheless a beautiful bird.

The archetypal "seagull," this species is the most widely distributed and abundant gull in the Northern Hemisphere. It is very adaptable to the changes being wrought to the marine and coastal environment by humans.

APPEARANCE
Length 25 inches. Wingspan 58 inches. A large, "typical" gull. By its fourth year the adult is overall white with a light slate gray back and pinkish legs. Large bill is yellow with an orange spot near the end. Winter adults have a mottled brown and dirty white plumage. Younger adults have a somewhat mottled appearance and juveniles are brownish.

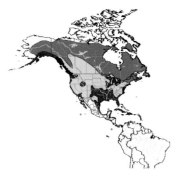
The range of the herring gull

HABITAT

Found along virtually all North American coasts. Does not shy away from coastal areas that are highly populated by humans. Found in great numbers in large urban harbors or busy fishing ports. Also found on coastal islands, as well as inland on lakes, ponds, rivers, marshes, sloughs and other wetland areas.

BEHAVIOR

Usually observed in large noisy flocks. Forages by picking food items off the ground or out of the water. A consummate scavenger. In this role it "cleans" up the shorelines of the coast, lakes, and rivers by taking stranded or dead organisms. Some feed at landfills and dumps, as well as on offal from fishing boats and fish processing plants. A powerful, graceful flier that seems to relish taking wing during storms.

CALLS

Has a variety of calls including the commonly heard *kack-kack-kack* and a *kyow-kyow-kyow* bugling.

FOOD

The herring gull is omnivorous and will eat just about anything it finds. This ability to adapt to a variety of foods no doubt contributes to its success as a species. Fish, crustaceans, mollusks, insects, sea urchins, young birds, eggs, amphibians and a variety of other animals are taken. Also eats seeds and berries during times when other foods are in short supply. Frequently scavenges.

FAMILY LIFE

Monogamous pair. Generally nests in colonies on islands along the coast or in lakes. Some colonies are very large. Male and female build a ground nest of grasses, seaweed, mosses and other materials, which is lined with grass and feathers. Will occasionally nest on cliffs or in trees if suitable ground sites are unavailable. The typical clutch of three eggs is incubated by both parents for 24 to 28 days. The precocial young leave the nest within a few hours of hatching and can fly at about 35 days, but are fed by the parents for some time after that. One brood per year.

An immature herring gull shows its mottled plumage

MIGRATION
Migratory over its northern and western breeding range. Many winter in the southern United States and along the west coast of the continent. In eastern North America, from the Great Lakes to the Atlantic coast, it is resident year-round.

CONSERVATION CONCERNS
Species status overall in North America is secure in the United States and secure in Canada. Extremely abundant with a growing population.

RELATED SPECIES
Very similar in appearance to the slightly smaller California gull. In addition to the herring gull, there are twelve other gulls in the genus *Larus* that breed in North America.

ICELAND GULL
Larus glaucoides

An Iceland gull in flight

This rather elegant, light-colored gull, which winters along the northeast coast of Canada and the United States, breeds in North America only on southern Baffin Island and smaller nearby islands in the Canadian Arctic. It is rather poorly known from a scientific standpoint. Despite its name, it does not breed in Iceland.

APPEARANCE
Length 23 inches. Wingspan 54 inches. Paler overall than most gulls. Light gray back and wings; the rest of the body is white. Light yellow eye with a red eye-ring; relatively small bill with a small spot near the tip of the lower mandible. Pinkish legs and feet. Easily distinguished from the herring gull by the absence of black on the wings. The North American race, known as the "Kumlien's form," tends to have gray stripes toward the tips of the undersides of the wings.

HABITAT

During the winter, Iceland gulls are found along the Atlantic coast from Newfoundland to North Carolina. Here they frequent fishing piers, harbors, coves and inlets, as well as more open coasts. Some birds winter on the eastern Great Lakes and the St. Lawrence River. In the breeding season they are found around their nesting colonies on the steep cliffs of southern Baffin Island and other areas of the eastern Arctic.

The range of the Iceland gull

BEHAVIOR

Forages largely by taking food items from the surface of the sea. Often fishes somewhat in the manner of a tern; it will scan an area from the air and on finding suitable prey will fly low, pick the fish directly from the water and occasionally land momentarily to secure it before taking wing again. Will also swim around on the surface pecking prey from the water. Food usually swallowed while in flight. Known to prey on young thick-billed murre chicks and eggs at breeding colonies in the eastern Arctic. Will follow fishing boats along with other gull species. Will also feed along the shore in shallow water. Less inclined to feed at garbage dumps than some other gull species. Quite agile at walking or running on land. Flight is typically gull-like, direct and fairly fast on steady, deeply beating wings.

CALLS

Calls are shriller than herring gull's. Performs a typically gull-like *kee-ah, kee-ah* or a *kee-yor, kee-yor, kee-yow, kee-yow* among other sounds.

FOOD

Diet consists primarily of fish including capelin and sand lance. Also eats a variety of invertebrates such as shrimp, crabs, marine worms, bivalve shellfish and urchins. Young seabirds (murres) and their eggs are sometimes also taken. Known to consume small amounts of plant matter.

FAMILY LIFE

Breeding biology is not well known. Monogamous pair. Nests in colonies. Nest is made of moss, other coarse vegetation and turf, lightly lined with grass or feathers and usually located on a cliff ledge. The typical clutch of one to three eggs is incubated by both sexes for 24 to 26 days. The semi-precocial young are fed by both parents for 24 to 29 days. One brood per year.

MIGRATION

Migration pattern of Canadian-breeding Kumlien's form is poorly known. Migration appears largely to be a movement between summer breeding areas to areas of open ocean known as polynyas where the birds can feed in winter. Unknown what proportion of the birds that breed in the eastern Canadian Arctic actually migrate south to winter along the eastern seaboard of North America. Many of these birds are immature. Spring migrants usually arrive back on their breeding grounds between late April and mid-June (the latter in the high Arctic). Fall migration generally occurs between mid-August and late September.

CONSERVATION CONCERNS

Species status overall is vulnerable in the United States and secure in Canada.

RELATED SPECIES

Some scientists believe the Iceland gull and the Thayer's gull should be considered the same species. One of thirteen gull species that breed in North America belonging to the genus *Larus*.

Iceland gulls can be distinguished from species such as the ring-billed, great black-backed and herring gulls by the lack of black wing tips

WESTERN GULL
Larus occidentalis

A western gull

This ubiquitous, large, dark-backed gull is an exclusively West Coast species that plays a similar ecological role as its somewhat larger East Coast counterpart, the great black-backed gull.

APPEARANCE
Length 25.5 inches. Wingspan 57 inches. Similar in size to the herring gull. Dark gray back and wings with black and white wing tips, white underparts. Legs and feet are pinkish; tail is white. Bill is yellow with a red spot near the tip of the lower mandible.

HABITAT
Inhabits a variety of coastal habitats including harbors, sandy beaches and intertidal zones, as well as areas in the vicinity of fish plants. Often feeds offshore. Also found around garbage dumps.

The range of the western gull

Frequently roosts on parking lots and other open areas located near the sea. Prefers islands for breeding sites.

BEHAVIOR

An opportunist that feeds in a wide variety of ways. Will float on the water and dip its bill, or do shallow lunges for surface prey. Will also do shallow plunge dives. In association with other marine birds, it will often follow seals, sea lions, and dolphins that are feeding. Follows fishing boats. Will walk in shallow water or on beaches and among rocks to find food items. Swallows small prey whole. Drops large shellfish from considerable heights onto the rocks below to break them open. Known to take milk directly from lactating seals. Flight is strong and graceful on steady beating wings. Soars on thermals and updrafts over cliffs.

CALLS

Performs a selection of twelve to fifteen calls. Often heard is a single *key-ow* call, as well as a variety of mews, yelps and a longer, more complex trumpeting call. Vocalizations are somewhat similar to the great black-backed gull's.

FOOD

A generalist that eats just about anything it can get a hold of. Diet includes saltwater fish and invertebrates, chicks and eggs, human garbage and carrion.

FAMILY LIFE

Monogamous pair. Nests in colonies on offshore islands. Both sexes participate in building the nest, which is a shallow cup constructed of coarse grasses, weeds and seaweeds. Nest is placed on the ground and usually located on a ledge, a slope or near a ridge. The typical clutch of three to four eggs is incubated for 25 to 32 days by both adults (largely the female). The semi-precocial young are fed by both parents for 29 to 32 days. One brood per year.

MIGRATION
Largely non-migratory. However, western gulls move a limited distance as they search for food. Birds that have dispersed to offshore feeding areas generally arrive back at their breeding areas in early to mid-spring. Most birds leave the area of their breeding colonies in October to move to these offshore feeding areas.

CONSERVATION CONCERNS
Species status overall in North America is secure in the United States. Only an infrequent visitor to Canada and does not breed there.

RELATED SPECIES
Most similar in appearance to the great black-backed and lesser black-backed gull, both eastern species.

The western gull is common on Pacific beaches

GREAT BLACK-BACKED GULL

Larus marinus

The largest of the gulls, the great black-backed is unmistakable with its very dark wings

This Atlantic coast species, the largest of all North American gulls, is nearly the size of a bald eagle. A powerful, aggressive gull, it is generally the dominant bird in its habitat.

APPEARANCE

Length 30 inches. Wingspan 65 inches. A very large black and white gull. Very dark gray back and upper wings, which get darker toward the ends; the very tips of the wings are white. Head, neck, tail and undersides are white. Yellow eye is surrounded by a thin red ring. The large, heavy bill is yellow with a red spot near the tip of the lower mandible. Legs are a fleshy pink.

HABITAT

Found along rocky shores, in intertidal zones and on mudflats along the northeast Atlantic coast. Not uncommon around harbors where it lingers near fish processing plants. Like the herring gull, this species frequents refuse dumps. Smaller populations are found in the eastern Great Lakes. Breeds on islands, rocky islets, headlands, barrier beaches and salt marshes. Occasionally breeds on lakes near the coast.

The range of the great black-backed gull

BEHAVIOR

An extremely opportunistic feeder, taking food in a variety of ways. Will commonly forage by walking along the water line or swimming in shallow water near shore to pick prey from the surface or dip into water to capture them. Also makes shallow plunge dives to a foot or two underwater for near-surface species. Follows fishing boats and eats discarded fish and other offal. Will feed on beaches and among rocks as it picks up crabs and other prey. Generally swallows small prey whole and will often break larger prey into smaller pieces or drop them from the air onto rocks to break shells open. Will pirate food items from smaller birds such as herring gulls and terns. Feeds at human garbage dumps. Flight is very strong and quite agile on heavy, deep wing beats.

CALLS

Less vocal than the herring gull. Most calls are similar to those of other gulls, but are somewhat lower in pitch. Most distinctive call is a deep *hur-ull.*

FOOD

Diet includes a wide variety of animals, plants and garbage. Eats any kind of fish small enough to capture. Also takes a variety of invertebrates such as crabs, sea urchins, squid, mussels and sea stars, as well as insects and worms. Eats colonial breeding birds and their eggs including puffins and Leach's storm-petrels, as well as larger species such as herring gulls and double-crested cormorants. Also consumes small mammals, fish offal and human garbage.

FAMILY LIFE

Monogamous pair. Generally nests in colonies. Both adults participate in building a shallow cup-shaped nest of seaweed, grass, moss
and debris, which is lined with fine grass. Nest is usually located on
top of a small pile of vegetation or seaweed. Sometimes a nest isn't
built if the area has a growth of thick sheltering grass. The typical
clutch of two to three eggs is incubated for 26 to 29 days by both
sexes. The semi-precocial young are fed by both parents for 49 to
56 days. One brood per year.

MIGRATION

Some populations are non-migratory. Others usually arrive at their
spring breeding grounds in March or April. Fall migration generally
occurs in September and October.

CONSERVATION CONCERNS

Species status overall is secure in the United States and secure in
Canada. Range is expanding on the Atlantic coast.

RELATED SPECIES

The two other largest gulls in North America are the western gull and
the glaucous gull, both of them smaller than the great black-backed.

A great black-backed gull spreading its nearly six-foot wingspan

BLACK-LEGGED KITTIWAKE

Rissa tridactyla

Black-legged kittiwakes squabble on a nesting ledge

Though it is a species of gull, the kittiwake is much more of a true seabird, spending most of its life out of sight of land.

APPEARANCE
Length 17 inches. Wingspan 36 inches. Typically gull-like in appearance, but somewhat more delicate. Back and wings are light gray, and the wing tips are black. Yellow bill is relatively small for a gull. Eyes are dark. Legs and feet are black and shorter than those of a typical gull.

HABITAT
In winter and during migration it is a pelagic species (only occasionally found on inland bodies of water). Its ability to drink salt water (among gulls, only the two kittiwake species can do this) enables it

The range of the black-legged kittiwake

to live well offshore in food-rich areas such as the Grand Banks. Often found at the edge of sea ice with northern fulmars and other seabirds. During the breeding season it is found near the coast, not far from its colonies, which are located on cliffs, sea stacks and isolated coastline areas that are free of predators.

BEHAVIOR

Forages by making low plunge dives from 3 to 20 feet above the surface and penetrating up to 3 feet underwater to capture prey. Often hovers close to the water momentarily before grabbing its prey. Also fishes by seizing prey while on the surface or by dipping its bill just underwater. Usually feeds in groups and tends to employ surface feeding rather than diving when flocks are large and dense. Occasionally follows fishing boats for offal. Its flight, which is extremely maneuverable and reminiscent of a tern, is very light and graceful on quick-beating, rather stiffly held wings. Moves with ease in storm winds, both along the cliffs of its breeding colony and over the open sea. While on the surface it must tread water with its feet to stay afloat. Sharp nails on its claws enable it to cling to the precipitous ledge at its nest site.

CALLS

Very vocal on its breeding colony. Named for its call, *kittiwake-kittiwake*. Also utters a low *awk-awk-awk* sound.

FOOD

Diet consists primarily of schooling surface fish such as sand lance, herring and capelin, as well as squid, krill and other small invertebrates. Will also take offal from fishing boats.

FAMILY LIFE

Monogamous pair. Nests in colonies that may contain tens of thousands of birds. Male and female build a deeply cupped nest of moss, seaweed and sod, which is cemented to a cliff ledge with mud. Nest often projects well over the lip of the ledge; there is little room for the occupants and most birds must face the cliff with their tails sticking out over the edge. The typical clutch of one to three eggs is incubated for 25 to 32 days by both sexes. The semi-precocial young remain in the nest for 34 to 58 days and are fed by both parents. One brood per year.

Although a member of the gull family, the kittiwake is truly a seabird and comes ashore only to breed

MIGRATION
Spring migrants arrive on their breeding grounds in March and April, although nest building may be delayed depending on weather and ice conditions. Fall migration generally occurs from late August to late September.

CONSERVATION CONCERNS
Species status overall in North America is secure in the United States and secure in Canada. Because kittiwakes nest in large colonies, breeding populations are vulnerable to oil spills in areas

where ship traffic occurs and also to changing fish distribution patterns due to climate change.

Black-legged kittiwakes breed on precarious ledges at sites located in the northern coastal areas of the continent

RELATED SPECIES

The only other kittiwake in North America is the red-legged species of Alaska. Both belong to the genus *Rissa*.

Did You Know?

One of the best places in the natural world to observe habitat selection is a typical seabird colony that contains several species. Most such colonies are arranged like multi-story apartment buildings with different species living on different levels. For example, guillemots are akin to ground-floor dwellers, breeding on low rocks nearest the water, while kittiwakes may live up one level on cliff ledges, with razorbills and murres just above them. Puffins usually nest in the sod high up at the edges of cliffs, and Leach's storm-petrels dig burrows among the trees.

ROYAL TERN

Sterna maxima

A royal tern on a southern beach in winter

The largest strictly coastal tern in North America, this "regal" species is a common sight along the shores of the mid-Atlantic, the Gulf of Mexico and the southern California coasts.

APPEARANCE
Length 20 inches. Wingspan 42 inches. The size of a small gull. Overall gray and white; gray back and wings, white underparts. Head has a full black cap during the breeding season and a partial cap in winter. Deeply forked tail, long pointed wings, and short black legs. Long chisel-shaped bill is red during breeding season and yellow-orange in winter.

HABITAT
Exclusively coastal, rarely seen inland. Inhabits warm water areas.

The range of the royal tern

Fishes along beaches (usually close to shore just beyond the surf zone), inlets, estuaries and lagoons, but is occasionally found 50 miles or more offshore. Only infrequently flies up creeks and other inland waterways in search of food. Breeds on isolated sandbars and barrier islands that are free of predators. Where natural breeding sites are unavailable, it will nest on islands created by the dredging of waterways and harbors.

BEHAVIOR

Forages by plunge diving into relatively clear, shallow water from a height of 15 to 30 feet, penetrating 3 to 6 feet below the surface to capture small fish. Dives are usually made within a few hundred feet of shore. A large flock of terns may gather in one place to hunt for schooling prey. Does not eat fish underwater but carries it crosswise in its bill to be eaten on shore or fed to its chick. Is known to fly considerable distances from its nest to find food. Notorious for stealing fish from the open bill pouches of pelicans. Rests on beaches and sandbars with other species of terns and gulls. Flight is direct with deep, flapping wing beats. Quite light on the wing, but less so than the common and Arctic terns.

A royal tern in breeding plumage in flight

CALLS
Has a variety of calls, the most common being the familiar *kee-yeer*, which is heard when the bird is foraging. Also utters a simple *kaak* among other less often heard calls.

FOOD
An opportunistic feeder that eats a wide variety of prey. May switch from one primary food species to another depending on abundance. Diet consists primarily of silversides, anchovies, sardines (in the Pacific), menhaden and other small fish. Also takes invertebrates such as shrimp and crabs.

FAMILY LIFE
Monogamous pair. Nests in colonies, often mixed with other species of terns. Male and female build the nest, which is a scrape in the sand on the beach. Nest is sometimes lined with bits of shells, fish bones and other debris. The typical clutch of one or two eggs is incubated by both adults for 20 to 31 days. The semi-precocial young are fed by both parents for 28 to 35 days. Young may remain with parents for up to 8 months or more. One brood per year.

MIGRATION
Spring migrants usually arrive on their breeding ground in March and April. Fall migration generally occurs between July and October.

CONSERVATION CONCERNS
Species status in North America is secure in the United States. Species does not occur in Canada, except as an accidental visitor. Destruction of suitable coastal habitat is an ever-present threat.

RELATED SPECIES
Nearest in size to the large Caspian tern, which is less exclusively coastal. One of thirteen species of terns occurring in North America that belong to the genus *Sterna*.

COMMON TERN

Sterna hirundo

A common tern is buoyant in flight

Light as a butterfly on the wing, the common tern seems at one with the air as it puts on a display of aerial agility and grace over the estuaries, beaches and shoals of the continent's coasts. However graceful it may appear on the wing, this bird is also one of the most aggressive and noisy inhabitants of the seashore.

APPEARANCE
Length 12 inches. Wingspan 30 inches. Overall sleek appearance. Though sometimes mistakenly referred to as a "mackerel gull," this tern is actually much smaller than most gulls and is much finer in build. Back is light gray, with whitish gray underparts. Large head with a distinctive black cap and nape and a long, thin, red bill that usually has a black tip. (The black tip is one way to distinguish it from the Arctic tern which has an all-red bill.) Short red

legs. Swallow-like tail is long and heavily forked. Slender pointed wings have darkened tips.

HABITAT

Breeds throughout the Northern Hemisphere and winters in the Southern Hemisphere. During the summer breeding season in North America, the common tern is found along the Atlantic coast where it favors barrier islands, estuaries and inlets, shoals, sandbars and areas with currents such as tide rips. Breeding islands are usually rocky in the northern part of its coastal range, and sandy in the southern part. Will often nest on islands

The range of the common tern

that are some distance from the shore. Inland they are found on lakes and large freshwater marshes. They also nest in the Great Lakes.

BEHAVIOR

Forages primarily by plunge diving. Will hover and hold its position over potential prey until it is within striking distance, then dives into the water from a height of up to 20 feet to capture the fish near the surface. Usually penetrates the water no deeper than a foot or two. Watching a flock of terns fishing over a shoal of small fish such as capelin can be an exciting experience. Also dives, swoops and dips bill into the water to grab food without landing. Birds with an established territory will often dive for food from a boat, bridge, jetty or other perch. Not a strong swimmer. Spends little time actually resting on the water, and rarely captures food from this position. Common terns often steal fish from other terns on the nesting colony. Extremely agile in the air, the common tern's flight is buoyant and graceful on deeply flapping wings.

CALLS

One of the most vociferous of North American birds, the common tern is best known for its grating, loud two-part descending *key-ar-r-r-r*. Also utters a variety of *kik-kik* notes and a *chip*.

FOOD

Diet is made up primarily of small fish up to about 6 inches long. In coastal areas it includes such species as sand lance, capelin, herring, shad, pollock, Atlantic mackerel and hake. Also takes a variety of shrimp, crabs and other small crustaceans. Birds that breed inland on freshwater environments eat small fish such as minnows, smelts and sticklebacks. Insects are also an important part of the diet.

FAMILY LIFE

Monogamous pair. Nests in colonies, some of which have thousands of pairs. Both sexes construct the nest, a simple depression in sand or gravel that is lined with grass, shells, seaweed and other vegetation. Nests are usually in the open, but are occasionally placed among grass or other vegetation. Colonies are placed on the upper part of beaches, on isolated peninsulas or on flat islands. The typical clutch of three eggs is incubated by both the male and female for 21 to 27 days. The semi-precocial young are fed by both adults. They make their first flight after 27 days and may remain with their parents for up to 2 months. One brood, rarely two broods per year.

A group of common terns gathered at the shore

A common tern hovering over the water before diving

MIGRATION

Spring migrants usually arrive en masse on their breeding grounds between mid-April and mid-May. Fall migration generally occurs in July and August with the birds congregating for some time before flying south later in the fall to their wintering range. Although they are long-range migrants, and many of them winter in South America, common terns are much less traveled than their close counterpart, the Arctic tern.

CONSERVATION CONCERNS

Species status overall in North America is secure in the United States and secure in Canada. Though its numbers have rebounded greatly, the common tern was nearly hunted to extinction in the late 1800s and early 1900s to supply feathers to the millinery trade. The harvesting of its eggs for food likely also contributed to the crash. Terns are still hunted for food on their wintering grounds in South America. Current threats in North America include rising sea levels and extreme weather caused by global warming, which can flood nesting areas that are located just above the high tide mark. Pollution and competition with herring gulls for nesting sites have also affected the tern population.

RELATED SPECIES

The common tern is one of thirteen tern species in North America that belong to the genus *Sterna*.

ARCTIC TERN

Sterna paradisaea

The Arctic tern is highly agile in flight

One of the migratory champions of the bird world, the Arctic tern sees more hours of daylight than any other animal. Its global peregrinations take it from the long days of northern summers in the Arctic where it breeds to the equally long days of southern summers around Antarctica. With an annual round trip of some 25,000 miles and a life span of over 30 years, this little species may migrate 750,000 miles in a lifetime, not including day-to-day foraging flights.

APPEARANCE

Length 12 inches. Wingspan 31 inches. Although similar in appearance to the common tern, it has a more deeply forked tail that extends slightly beyond the tips of its folded wings. Completely red bill is shorter than the common tern's and lacks the black tip. Head appears smaller and underparts are also somewhat darker.

HABITAT

In summer its coastal haunts are similar to those of the common tern, and although their breeding ranges overlap somewhat in Atlantic Canada, the Arctic's range is farther north on average. Inhabits estuaries and marine waters, often extending out to sea 10 miles or more. Colony is usually located on a beach, a grassy shoreline or an offshore island. Often observed resting with other tern species on sandbars and beaches. Inland nesting habitat is usually on treeless tundra that is surrounded by lakes and ponds. The pack ice around Antarctica is its winter home.

The range of the Arctic tern

BEHAVIOR

Foraging habits are similar to the common tern. Primarily a plunge diver, taking fish from just below the surface. Before plunging, will fly back and forth over the water with head pointed downward as it looks for prey. Also "dips" food items from the surface with its bill while on the wing. On breeding grounds will often snap insects up in mid-air. Bounding upward with each downbeat of its wings, its flight is even more buoyant than the common tern's. Does not normally swim on the surface. Very short legs make walking somewhat awkward and the bird has a pronounced waddling gait. An Arctic tern will often feed offshore where prey is driven to the surface by predatory fish. Feeds on scraps brought to the surface by marine-diving foragers such as seals and whales. Will pirate fish from puffins and other small diving birds.

CALLS

Very similar to the common tern's, but generally a little harsher and higher pitched.

FOOD

Diet consists mostly of sand lance, herring, young cod and pollock, smelt, capelin, small mackerel and other small fish. Also takes small crabs, shrimp, krill and other crustaceans, as well as insects.

FAMILY LIFE

Monogamous pair. Nests in colonies and occasionally in single pairs. Both sexes prepare the nest, which is little more than a depression in sand, gravel or moss, lined with small debris, grass or broken shells. Nest is located on a small coastal island, sand spit or dune area. Also found on islands or along the shores of northern lakes, ponds and marshes. The typical clutch of two eggs is incubated by both adults for 20 to 24 days. Semi-precocial young leave the nest after about 2 days but are tended and fed by both parents for up to 60 days. One brood per year.

Arctic terns are one of the champions of long-distance migration, flying from the Arctic to the Antarctic and back again every year

MIGRATION

Arctic terns perform one of the longest annual migrations of any bird. After leaving breeding areas in the Northern Hemisphere soon after young have fledged (usually no later than August), they migrate to the ocean around Antarctica where they overwinter. Returning migrants generally arrive back at their North American breeding grounds from mid-May to late June (the latter in the high Arctic).

CONSERVATION CONCERNS

Species status overall in North America is secure in the United States and secure in Canada. Nearly hunted to extinction for feathers to supply the eastern U.S. hat-making industry in the late 1800's. Still subject to intense egg gathering by humans in high Arctic areas, especially in Greenland. Population may be threatened as climate change alters the distribution of sea ice and prey species in the Arctic and Antarctic.

RELATED SPECIES

One of thirteen tern species in North America that belong to the genus *Sterna*. Quite similar to the common and roseate tern.

BLACK SKIMMER

Rynchops niger

A black skimmer flying low over the water, hunting for fish

Though resembling a tern, the black skimmer, with its spectacular and completely unique feeding strategy, is unlikely to be mistaken for any other species in North America.

APPEARANCE

Length 18 inches. Wingspan 44 inches. A slender bird, the size and general shape of a tern. Wings very long relative to its body. Back, wings and back of head and neck are black. Front of face, neck, breast and underparts are white. Large black-tipped orange-red bill is compressed vertically like a knife blade; lower mandible is one-third longer than the upper one. Very short orange-red legs. Slightly forked tail.

HABITAT

Inhabits coastal beaches, saltwater lagoons, salt marshes, sandbars, inlets, estuaries, salt marsh creeks and occasionally rivers and freshwater marshes. Generally feeds in very shallow water.

The range of the black skimmer

BEHAVIOR

The defining characteristic of the black skimmer is its method of foraging. It flies just inches above the surface of a lagoon or other body of shallow water with its bill open and its long lower mandible slicing through the water to capture fish. The upper mandible can be seen snapping shut on any prey scooped up by the lower. This is one of the most finely coordinated maneuvers in the avian world and has to be seen to be appreciated. Forages largely at night, but also early in the morning and in the late evening (only occasionally mid-day) when fish and other prey are nearer to the surface. Usually observed in small flocks. Though its flight on long, slender wings is graceful and

A black skimmer slices through the water with its long lower mandible as it forages for small fish

buoyant, skimmers are relatively weak fliers. However, flocks have the ability to synchronize beautifully in flight the way shorebirds do. Often rests on beaches and sandbars with terns and gulls.

CALLS
Gives a low, grating *kuk-kuk-kuk* barking call.

FOOD
Diet consists primarily of small surface-feeding fish, but will occasionally take shrimp and other invertebrates.

The black skimmer is extremely efficient at flying just inches above the water's surface

FAMILY LIFE
Monogamous pair. Nests in small colonies, occasionally with terns or gulls. Both sexes build a simple unlined scrape nest in sand or gravel, making no attempt to conceal it. Nest is usually located on sandy islands or sandbars. The typical clutch of four eggs is incubated by both adults for 21 to 23 days. The semi-precocial young are fed by both adults for 23 to 25 days. One brood per year.

MIGRATION
Largely a non-migratory permanent resident throughout most of its North American range. Some northerly birds that nest on the mid-Atlantic coast are migratory and usually arrive on their summer breeding grounds in April and May. Fall migration generally occurs in September and October. Large permanent population in South America.

CONSERVATION CONCERNS
Overall species status in North America is secure in the United States. Because it generally nests on low-lying sandy areas, the black skimmer may be extremely vulnerable to rising sea levels caused by global warming.

RELATED SPECIES
The only species of the genus *Rynchops* in North America. Three species of skimmer are found worldwide.

AUKS

COMMON MURRE
Uria aalge

A pair of common murres

The common murre (known as the guillemot in Europe and turre in Newfoundland) is the largest and heaviest of the auks. It is one of the most abundant marine birds in the seas surrounding North America with a population of up to 9 million pairs. Humans living in northern coastal areas have eaten murres and their eggs for thousands of years. It is one of the most studied seabirds in the world.

APPEARANCE
Length 17 inches. Wingspan 26 inches. A crow-sized bird with a black back, neck, throat and head; white belly. Short, thick neck. The thin black bill ends at a sharp point. Two forms of the species exist, one with no white markings on the face, and an exclusively eastern "bridled" form that has a thin white ring around the eye,

197

The range of the common murre

and a line leading from the back of the eye down the neck. Stout black legs are rear-set for efficient swimming.

HABITAT

In winter usually found along the coast from about 5 miles offshore to the edge of the continental shelf. In summer tends to remain in the area of its breeding colonies, which are located on flat, rocky offshore islands or sea cliffs.

BEHAVIOR

Forages by surface diving to capture prey in its bill, descending to a maximum of just over 200 feet below the surface, with average dives of between about 60 and 160 feet. Deepest recorded dive is about 560 feet. Propels itself by using its wings to "fly" underwater in pursuit of prey. It is thought that common murres ascend through large schools of fish from beneath. Feeds both in flocks and individually. Because it has a very small wing area relative to body weight, it must beat its wings extremely rapidly and maintain high speeds to stay airborne. Flies low over the water and changes direction frequently and rapidly. Groups fly in lines. Can only get airborne by diving off a cliff or by rapidly running across water. Floats high in the water. Moving on land is awkward as it shuffles along upright on its bent legs.

CALLS

Silent when not on the breeding colony. Utters a variety of growls and low moans at nest site.

FOOD

Diet consists primarily of fish, including capelin, small pollock, cod, herring, smelt, sand lance, sardine and anchovy, depending on the location. Also consumes shrimp and other invertebrates.

FAMILY LIFE

Monogamous pair. Nests in very large, dense colonies of up to hundreds of thousands of pairs. The single egg is placed on bare rock on an island or on a cliff ledge and is incubated by both adults for 32 to 33 days. The semi-precocial chick is fed by both parents for 19 to 21 days before it leaves the nest. Virtually all the chicks in a colony leave their nests in a mass synchronized departure that occurs over just a few days. During this perilous time, the chick must leap from the cliff ledge with only half-formed wings, or tumble down a grassy slope to reach the water. Once on the ocean the chick is tended by the male, which feeds it and shows it good foraging areas for a month or two. One brood per year, but will lay a second egg if the first fails.

Distinctive in its black and white plumage, a common murre climbs a rocky slope on its breeding ground

MIGRATION

Whether a population is migratory depends on the latitude of the colony. Arctic birds avoid the sea ice by migrating to areas where they can feed in open water in the winter. Timing of movement away from breeding areas is probably dictated by the formation of sea ice in the fall or early winter, with a return as the sea ice begins to break up in the spring. Birds that nest in less ice-prone areas may stay in the vicinity of the colony, dispersing to find food.

CONSERVATION CONCERNS

Species status overall in North America is secure in the United States and secure in Canada. Despite this, common murres are highly susceptible to being killed by oil spills. The Exxon Valdez disaster in Alaska in 1989 resulted in the deaths of nearly 200,000 murres. And, tens of thousands are killed each year after being fouled in oil slicks caused by ships illegally cleaning out their bilges at sea. Though steps have been made to reduce such tragedies, bird mortality remains high.

RELATED SPECIES

The common murre's closest relative and only other member of the genus *Uria* is the very similar thick-billed murre. Other closely related species include the razorbill and the extinct great auk.

Did You Know?

One of the greatest threats to seabirds and coastal birds is an oil spill. Unlike their terrestrial cousins, water-loving birds must place themselves either in, on or at the edge of the sea to find food for survival. While terrestrial oil and chemical spills are usually confined to a relatively small area, such spills on the water can disperse widely and quickly on the surface. It takes only a few drops of oil to destroy the insulating qualities of a seabird's plumage, and the result is usually a slow death from hypothermia. As tragic as large disastrous events such as the Exxon Valdez spill are, many more birds die from the unregulated dumping of bilge water at sea, which puts thousands of tons of oil into the oceans every year. An estimated 300,000 seabirds die this way every year off the southern coast of Newfoundland alone.

RAZORBILL

Alca torda

Razorbill auks on a cliff at their breeding colony

The razorbill is the closest living relative to the extinct great auk of the North Atlantic. It has one of the smaller populations of the auks in North America, with some 40,000 pairs.

APPEARANCE

Length 17 inches. Wingspan 26 inches. Crow-sized. Black and white, it looks as if it is wearing a tuxedo. Back, wings, tail, head and feet are black; belly is white. Heavy, blunt bill is black with a thin vertical line near the tip; thin horizontal white line running from the base of the bill to the eye. Wings are short and narrow and the tail is long and pointed. In winter the white on the belly extends to the chin and the horizontal line disappears.

HABITAT

During the summer it is found in northern Atlantic coastal waters in the vicinity of its breeding colonies. Less pelagic than the common and thick-billed murres, razorbills will breed in large estuaries such as the St. Lawrence River in Quebec, in addition to more open coasts. In winter many birds move farther from land, and some of the population goes south along the eastern seaboard of the U.S. A large wintering population concentrates in the Gulf of Maine and the outer Bay of Fundy.

The range of the razorbill

BEHAVIOR

Forages by diving and pursuing fish underwater. Propels itself rapidly by "flying" underwater with half-open wings. Dives usually last about 30 seconds and are an average maximum of about 80 feet deep. Smaller fish are swallowed whole underwater while larger ones are brought to the surface to be eaten. Like the puffin, the razorbill can hold several fish crosswise in its bill, which are then brought to its young. A strong surface swimmer using its large feet as paddles. Moves about on breeding site in an upright posture, somewhat penguin-like (though they are not related, since penguins are Southern Hemisphere species). Flight is rapid on quickly beating wings. Highly maneuverable compared to other auk species. Must flap wings vigorously and run along the water to get airborne. It may have the quickest flight of all the auk species, with speeds approaching or exceeding 50 miles per hour.

CALLS

Silent at sea. On its breeding colony it performs various guttural grunts and occasional whistles.

FOOD

Diet consists primarily of sand lance, capelin, sculpins, herring and other small fish. Invertebrates are also taken. Chicks eat fish exclusively.

FAMILY LIFE
Monogamous pair. Nests in relatively small colonies, sometimes with other species. Both sexes build a nest located on a cliff ledge, under an overhang or among boulders and rocks on an offshore island that is safe from mammalian predators. Nest site is often well concealed and partly enclosed. Nest is lined with bits of vegetation, feathers, seashells, small rocks and other debris. The single egg is incubated by both adults for 35 to 37 days. The semi-precocial young remains in the nest for 14 to 25 days where it is fed by both parents. The male feeds the young at sea for 2 months after it leaves the nest. One brood per year.

MIGRATION
Migration pattern for North American razorbills is not well known. Birds breeding in northern areas that experience sea ice may be more migratory than those that live in ice-free areas such as the Bay of Fundy and the Gulf of Maine. Spring migrants are thought to arrive on their breeding grounds between mid-March and mid-May (the latter in more northerly areas). Fall migration generally begins in August.

CONSERVATION CONCERNS
Species status overall in North America is critically imperiled in the United States and secure in Canada. In the U.S., the razorbill has one of the smallest breeding populations of any seabird with only about 300 nesting pairs, located in Maine. Razorbills are considered to be very vulnerable to

A conservation status map for the razorbill

oil spills, especially where they congregate in winter in the Gulf of Maine/Bay of Fundy and where they breed in the Gulf of St. Lawrence, both locations on or near major shipping lanes.

RELATED SPECIES
One of twelve species regularly breeding in North America that belongs to the family *Alcidae*. The sole species in the genus *Alca*.

Did You Know?

Although we now know the group of flightless seabirds living in the Southern Hemisphere as penguins, the bird that was first called a "penguin" was the now-extinct great auk of the North Atlantic (hence its scientific name of *Pinguinus impennis*). This remarkable flightless bird, the largest of all the auk species, stood some 30 inches tall, and bred in enormous numbers from northern Europe to the Gulf of St. Lawrence. Unfortunately, it was an easy victim for fishermen and other mariners who often visited its colonies to kill it for meat and to take its eggs. The great auk was driven to extinction by the mid-1850s. Its closest living relative is the razorbill.

BLACK GUILLEMOT

Cepphus grylle

The black guillemot is also known as a "sea pigeon" because of its small size

This small, slender-bodied seabird is commonly observed in coastal areas near the shore. Known as the sea pigeon for its superficial resemblance to doves (it has very nearly the same size and proportion as a mourning dove), guillemots are more often found singly or in very small groups than other members of the auk family.

APPEARANCE
Length 14 inches. Wingspan 23 inches. Overall black with large white patch on the wing. Underwings are white. Conspicuous bright red legs and feet are placed rearward on the body. Moderately long, thin, pointed bill. Wintering adults and all juveniles are overall white or whitish gray with a dark mottled back. White wing patch and red feet still apparent in winter.

HABITAT

Found almost exclusively near shore where it fishes for prey in shallow water. In winter it can be found offshore near ice floes. Often seen diving in protected coves where its bottom-dwelling prey is abundant. Prefers rocky shores and off-shore islands for breeding.

The range of the black guillemot

BEHAVIOR

Forages by diving, generally to depths of up to 100 feet, but also known to fish in water less than 3 feet deep. Propels itself like other auks, by using its wings to "fly" underwater, perhaps using its feet as rudders. Remains underwater for more than a minute on average and sometimes over two minutes. Feeds primarily on the bottom, often flipping over small stones as it searches for fish. Occasionally captures prey in mid-water. When coastal areas freeze over, the black guillemot moves to offshore areas where it will feed around ice floes. Flight is strong and direct on rapidly beating wings and generally occurs fairly close to the surface of the water. An efficient surface swimmer, paddling with its feet and

Black guillemots are black with white patches in summer

occasionally using its wings to skitter across the water. Able to walk, run and hop surprisingly well in an upright position. Also pushes itself along the ground on its belly.

CALLS
Usually silent, however it utters a weak, high-pitched wheezing whistle, *feee*.

In winter the plumage of the black guillemot becomes largely white

FOOD
Diet consists largely of bottom-dwelling fish such as rock gunnels, small sculpins, shannies, cod and blennies. A diverse array of invertebrates is also taken.

FAMILY LIFE
Monogamous pair. Generally breeds in small colonies (although some colonies in the Arctic may contain up to 10,000 pairs) or occasionally as individual pairs. Both adults participate in preparing a nest that is lined with small pebbles. It is generally located among rubble, under a rock or in crevices on talus slopes, cliff faces

or clay banks. Occasionally will nest on a flat shoreline if sufficient cover is available, or in the crevices of artificial breakwaters. The typical clutch of two eggs is incubated by both sexes for approximately 30 days. The semi-precocial chicks are fed by both parents and remain in the nest for 34 to 39 days. One brood per year.

MIGRATION

Generally non-migratory, but in winter some temperate-latitude birds move south along the Atlantic coast as far as New Jersey. In winter, high Arctic breeders disperse offshore to open water at the edge of ice floes to feed.

CONSERVATION CONCERNS

Species status overall in the United States is apparently secure. In

the coterminous U.S., it breeds only in Maine, with a population of approximately 2,700 pairs. Some 2,000 pairs also breed on the northern coast of Alaska. Species status in Canada is secure with a large population widely distributed throughout Atlantic Canada and the Arctic.

A conservation status map for the black guillemot

RELATED SPECIES

The quite similar pigeon guillemot of the West Coast belongs to the same genus *Cepphus*.

ATLANTIC PUFFIN

Fratercula arctica

An Atlantic puffin "stretches" its wings before take off from a cliff at its breeding colony

With its comic stubby stature, black and white "tuxedo" plumage and large, brightly colored bill, the Atlantic puffin is the most recognized species of seabird in the Northern Hemisphere. Despite this, relatively little is known of its life history outside the breeding season.

APPEARANCE

Length 12 inches. Wingspan 21 inches. Unmistakable appearance. Black back, wings, back of neck and crown with white undersides. Large head with very large, heavy triangular bill that is bright orange with a blue-gray crescent at its base. Face is light gray and the throat sports a black collar that is contiguous with the rest of the black plumage. Legs and feet are bright orange. In winter the white face darkens, while the bill becomes duller and shrinks in size as the outer bony plates are shed. The bright orange of the legs and feet become

The range of the Atlantic puffin

duller as well. The only other North American species that is very similar in appearance is the horned puffin. Distinguishing between them in the field is not necessary, however, since their ranges are on opposite sides of the continent and do not overlap.

HABITAT

Spends non-breeding season offshore, occasionally far from land beyond the continental shelf. During the breeding season, the puffin is found inhabiting the near-shore waters in the vicinity of its nesting colony. In North America, all colonies are located on islands where conditions are suitable for digging burrows. Normally found in sloped grassy areas or near the tops of cliffs. On one island in Nova Scotia, puffins have resorted to nesting in holes in the face of the cliffs after gulls took over their nesting sites on flat, grassy areas.

BEHAVIOR

Forages by surface diving into schools of small fish. May dive to over 200 feet deep on occasion, but generally shallower. Remains submerged for about 30 seconds. Uses wings as flippers to "fly" underwater and uses its feet as rudders. Often catches several small fish per dive. Small fish are usually swallowed underwater, while larger fish are held sideways in the bill (the archetypal image of the puffin just returned home with a large bunch of fish stuffed in its bill!). A compromise has been struck between the efficiency of its wings for swimming and for flying. As a result, they have become short and provide relatively little lift in the air, resulting in flight that is rapid and direct on whirring, rapidly beating wings. Walks quite upright with a waddle.

CALLS

A variety of groans, moans and growls are uttered at the nest site, most notably a growling *ow-ahh-ahh-ahh*. Not known if it vocalizes at sea. Chicks make a variety of whines and chipping sounds.

FOOD

Takes a variety of small fish, including sand lance, capelin, herring, hake, Arctic cod and possibly lantern fish, among others. Also eats invertebrates such as squid and marine worms, as well as small crustaceans.

An Atlantic puffin in flight with a bill full of small fish for its young

FAMILY LIFE

Monogamous pair. Breeds in colonies that range from dozens to thousands of pairs. Male excavates a burrow nest in sod or beneath rocks, which extends horizontally into the ground for about 3 feet and ends in a small chamber that is lined with grass or feathers. Both adults incubate the single egg for 39 to 45 days. The semi-precocial chick is fed by both parents for 38 to 44 days before they abandon it and move out to sea. One brood per year.

MIGRATION

Migratory behavior is not well known. Moves offshore during

non-breeding season. Spring migrants generally arrive on their breeding grounds in mid- to late April. Fall migration usually begins between late August and late September.

CONSERVATION CONCERNS

Species status overall for North America is critically endangered in the United States and secure in Canada. There are only approximately 600 pairs breeding in the United States, all of them in the state of Maine. Over 300,000 pairs nest at dozens of sites throughout eastern Canada, about two-thirds of them at one colony on Newfoundland's Avalon Peninsula.

A conservation status map for the Atlantic puffin

RELATED SPECIES

There are three puffin species in North America: the Atlantic on the East Coast and the tufted and horned puffins on the West. All three belong to the genus *Fratercula*.

An Atlantic puffin lands

HORNED PUFFIN
Fratercula corniculata

A horned puffin at its breeding colony

This larger West Coast counterpart to the Atlantic puffin is relatively poorly known from a scientific standpoint due to its remote nesting locations in the northern Pacific Ocean.

APPEARANCE
Length 14.5 inches. Wingspan 22 inches. Larger than the similar Atlantic puffin. Black back and wings, white underparts; large white cheek patch and black cap. Bill is similar in shape and proportion to the Atlantic puffin, but less colorful with a yellow base and an orange tip. Eye is dark with an orange ring. A fleshy "horn" extends from the top of the eye to the crown. Orange legs and feet. Bill and cheek patch of adults are duller in winter.

HABITAT

Strictly marine. Although its range overlaps that of the tufted puffin somewhat, this species tends to breed farther north. Is found far offshore beyond the continental shelf over the deep oceanic waters of the central North Pacific during the non-breeding season, although some birds overwinter around the Aleutian Islands. Even in summer, when it breeds on rocky, barren islands and sea cliffs on the mainland, it will often travel well out to sea to capture food. Many of its largest breeding colonies are located on remote, inaccessible offshore islands.

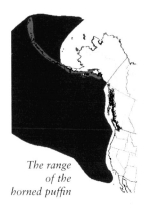

The range of the horned puffin

BEHAVIOR

Captures its food by diving much like other puffins. When foraging it propels itself by using its half-opened wings to "fly" rapidly underwater at up to 6 feet per second. Most dives are probably to a depth of less than 100 feet. It tends to pursue prey in mid-water instead of near the bottom. Swallows prey underwater, except for the small fish intended for its chick, which are carried crosswise in the bill in of five or more. If an abundance of prey is available, it will often forage in small flocks, sometimes in mixed associations with other seabird species. Walks with an upright stance and is relatively agile on the ground, scrambling over boulders and climbing cliffs. Flight is strong and direct on rapidly beating wings, but its maneuverability is poor. Mid-air collisions with other horned puffins at breeding colonies are not uncommon.

CALLS

Largely silent at sea. Utters a variety of growls and grunts in the breeding colony.

FAMILY LIFE

Monogamous pair. Nests in colonies. Both adults build the nest, which is generally located in a rock crevice, on a cliff or in a shallow burrow. Nest is occasionally lined with grass. The single egg is incubated by both sexes for 40 to 42 days. The semi-precocial chick is fed by both parents for 34 to 40 days. One brood per year.

MIGRATION

Although some birds stay in the vicinity of their breeding grounds in the Aleutian Islands and the Gulf of Alaska, most migrate to the central North Pacific to overwinter. Many horned puffins travel far from the continent where they will feed with truly pelagic species such as shearwaters and albatrosses. Spring migrants usually arrive back at the breeding colony from early May to early June (the latter for northernmost breeding colonies). Birds generally depart breeding colonies in September.

CONSERVATION CONCERNS

Species status overall in North America is secure in the United States (almost all horned puffins in North America nest in Alaska) and imperiled in Canada where its breeding population is small. Oil spills pose a major threat to horned puffins when they are on their breeding grounds in summer. However, in winter, when most oil spills occur inshore (due to bad weather), the birds are usually well out to sea. Mortality from high-seas gill nets or drift nets can be extreme—tens of thousands of horned puffins have been killed by them over the last few decades.

RELATED SPECIES

Its nearest relative is the very similar but smaller Atlantic puffin. All three puffin species belong to the genus *Fratercula*.

TUFTED PUFFIN
Fratercula cirrhata

A pair of tufted puffins in full breeding plumage

Compared to its clownlike cousins, the Atlantic and horned puffins, the tufted puffin, with its long blond feather tufts and bold white face mask, looks like the "bad boy" of its genus.

APPEARANCE
Length 15 inches. Wingspan 24 inches. The largest puffin; an overall black and white seabird the size of a common pigeon (rock dove). Distinctive long yellow feather tufts or plumes are unmistakable. White face. Bill is orange and less massive than those of the other puffin species. Eyes are yellow with a thin red ring. Orange legs and feet. The entire body is black, unlike other puffin species. Adults lose their head plumes in winter.

HABITAT

Exclusively marine. Lives along the Pacific coast of North America. Along with the horned puffin, it is essentially an open-ocean, offshore species. It spends its life ranging widely at sea from the Arctic to the coast of California, usually far from land beyond the continental slope. During the breeding season, the tufted puffin remains in the waters around its nesting colony. Colonies are located on steep-sided rocky islands and cliffs on the

The range of the tufted puffin

mainland. The breeding sites must be located in grassy slopes or in areas near the tops of cliffs that are suitable for digging burrows.

BEHAVIOR

Forages by surface diving and pursuing prey underwater where it propels itself by "flying" with half-open beating wings. Very rapid underwater swimmer. Most dives are probably less than 200 feet deep. Tends to capture prey nearer the bottom than other puffin species. Swallows prey underwater, except the small fish meant for chicks, which are carried sideways in the bill. Usually feeds in small groups, often in association with other fish-eating seabird species. Walks effectively using an upright stance and is comfortable clambering over rocks and climbing cliffs. Flight is rapid and direct on rapidly beating wings. More maneuverable than other puffin species. In flight it uses its feet to help it steer. Builds up speed by pattering across the water prior to takeoff. Displays little grace on its return to the nesting site, often crashing into obstacles upon landing.

CALLS

Silent at sea. Makes a variety of groaning and grunting noises on the breeding colony.

FOOD

Diet is made up of a combination of fish and invertebrates. When feeding for themselves, adults tend to take more invertebrates such

AUKS

as squid and shrimp. However, when obtaining food for their young, they take mostly fish such as anchovy, sand lance, young pollock and capelin.

A tufted puffin shows off its all-black body and the feather tufts that give it its name

FAMILY LIFE
Monogamous pair. Breeds in colonies. Both adults excavate a shallow burrow in soft turf, soil or peat and line the egg chamber with grass and feathers. The tunnel to the chamber can be from 2 to 10 feet long. Nest usually located on a grassy slope or on the top of a cliff. The single egg is incubated for 41 days by both sexes. The semi-precocial chick is fed by both parents for 45 days. One brood per year in the North, two broods in the South.

MIGRATION
Generally migrates from breeding areas in the northern Pacific to wintering areas in the north-central Pacific. Migratory populations arrive on their breeding colony between April and mid-June (the latter in more northerly areas). Breeding grounds usually vacated between September and late October. Some birds do not migrate,

while others that breed in high latitudes are merely pushed south-ward by the advancing winter sea ice.

CONSERVATION CONCERNS
Species status overall in North America is secure in the United States and vulnerable in Canada. The greatest immediate threat to tufted puffins comes from potential oil spills. Up to 13,000 birds may have been killed by the Exxon Valdez disaster in Prince William Sound, Alaska, in 1989. Drift nets present a great risk to seabirds and the tufted puffin is no exception, suffering a mortality of 15,000 to 30,000 birds per year during the 1990s.

RELATED SPECIES

There are three puffin species in North America, the Atlantic on the East Coast and the tufted and horned puffins on the West. All three belong to the genus *Fratercula*.

Did You Know?
Several different diving techniques are used by seabirds and coastal bird species. Puffins, murres and razorbills have quite small, short wings and use them as flippers to "fly" underwater. Gannets, terns and pelicans have long wings and are naturally buoyant because of hollow bones and air sacs in the body, so they partially rely on the momentum gained by entering the water at high speed to carry them beneath it. Loons, grebes and cor-morants employ a different strategy and hold their wings against their bodies while using powerful legs and webbed feet (lobed feet in the case of grebes) to propel themselves underwater.

CROSSROADS ON THE SEA:

THE FUTURE OF SEABIRDS

Twenty-five hundred miles southeast of Cape St. Mary's and six months later, I am again marveling at the grace of northern gannets as I watch them plunging into the sea in pursuit of fish off the Atlantic coast of Florida. They have left the North Atlantic winter storms behind for warmer climes and abundant food. Though well offshore and visible with the naked eye only as bright specks against the dark horizon, a spotting scope draws them into focus. With their wings held straight out behind them, they slice into the water at steep angles like javelins, sending small plumes of white-water into the air on entry.

Much nearer to shore, a squadron of brown pelicans patrols the surf zone along the seemingly endless beach before heading beyond

Brown pelicans cruising along the Atlantic coast of Florida

the breakers to perform their own variation on the plunge diving theme. These pelicans are southern counterparts to their northern cousins the gannets. Despite their very different appearance, they play a similar ecological role in the sea. In fact, both belong in the same order, the *Pelicaniformes*. Closer still, a flock of sanderlings, on a winter sabbatical from their high Arctic breeding grounds, is forced up the beach by a wave to scamper among several dozen royal terns and laughing gulls resting on the sand.

It is deserted here, except for the birds. It's too cold to swim in January, and a blustery nor'easter has kept even the beach walkers away. Canaveral National Seashore belongs to the wind today, its 24 miles of pristine sand running straight as a compass needle northwest to southeast, under steel-gray winter skies.

Sitting incongruously in the middle of the coastal marshlands a few miles to the south is the Kennedy Space Center at Cape Canaveral, its giant hangar and rocket gantries monuments to the space age and technological achievement. It was built at a time when exploring space seemed more important than understanding our own planet. For western civilization, it was in a way symbolic of a turning away from the world we had inherited to one we'd created. Our pathologically complex scientific-industrial society of today seems to have lost an understanding of its place on the earth, so self-obsessed have we become, to the exclusion of other living things on the planet. As the author Ursula

A flock of dunlins resting on a southern beach in January

The everlasting sea awaits a new day

K. LeGuin has written, "By climbing up into his head and shutting out every voice but his own, 'Civilized Man' has gone deaf…he can't hear the earth calling him child."

As the last large undeveloped stretch of coastline on the Atlantic coast of Florida, Canaveral National Seashore has a different, more enduring symbolism. It shows us the good that can come when we recognize that there is a world *outside* our own and we take real steps to ensure its continuance (and in doing so, ensuring our own). This place is just one of many crossroads in North America, a nexus of wintering ocean birds from the north and the south. Gannets, pelicans, sanderlings, terns and other seabird and coastal species have probably been crossing paths here for thousands of years before humans arrived on the scene. Their migratory tracks like stitches on the fabric of the biosphere, ocean birds around the world link distant places like Cape St. Mary's and Cape Canaveral together, making the ocean and its coasts one grand habitat. Gannets and pelicans, northern seas and the southern ones, ocean currents and climate, microscopic plankton and the sun, *everything* is linked somehow to everything else in the sea.

As we stand at a crossroads in the history of life in the sea, and indeed on earth, we are only now beginning to understand this concept of the interconnectedness of all life, no matter how disparate and detached its individual elements might appear.

SELECTED BIBLIOGRAPHY

Alsop, Jr., Fred J. *Birds of Canada*. Toronto: Dorling Kindersley Handbooks, 2002.

Armstrong, Edward A. *The Ethology of Bird Display and Bird Behavior*, rev. ed. New York: Dover Publications, 1965.

Askins, Robert A. *Restoring North America's Birds*. New Haven: Yale University Press, 2000.

Attenborough, David. *The Life of Birds*. Princeton: BBC Books, 1998.

Audubon, John James. *Audubon's Birds of America*, Popular edition. Toronto: The MacMillan Company, 1950.

Beletsky, Les. *Collins Birds of the World*. London: Collins, 2006.

Bent, Arthur Cleveland. *Life Histories of North American Gulls and Terns*, Part One. New York: Dover Edition, 1961. (Originally published 1921.)

Bird, David M. *The Bird Almanac*. Toronto: Key Porter Books, 1999.

Boag, David, and Mike Alexander. *The Atlantic Puffin*. Poole: Blandford Press, 1986.

Brooke, Michael, and Tim Birkhead. *The Cambridge Encyclopedia of Ornithology*. New York: Cambridge University Press, 1991.

Carwardine, Mark. *Birds in Focus*. London: Salamander Books, 1990.

Chapman, Frank M. *Bird Life*. New York: D. Appleton and Company, 1910.

Cornell Lab of Ornithology. *The Birds of North America Online*, 2004–2005. Ithaca: Cornell Lab of Ornithology, 2004–2005.

Dando, Mark, and Michael Burchett. Waller, Geoffrey, ed. *SeaLife: A Complete Guide to the Marine Environment*. Washington: Smithsonian Institution Press, 1996.

Ehrlich, Paul R. *The Machinery of Nature*. New York: Touchstone Books, 1986.

Ehrlich, Paul R., David S. Dobkin, and Darryl Wheye. *The Birder's Handbook*. New York: Fireside, 1988.

Erskine, Anthony J. *Atlas of Breeding Birds of the Maritime Provinces*. Halifax: Nimbus/Nova Scotia Museum, 1992.

Feduccia, Alan. *The Origin and Evolution of Birds,* 2nd ed. New Haven: Yale University Press, 1999.

Fish and Wildlife Service. *Migration of Birds, Circular 16*. Washington: Fish and Wildlife Service, US Dept. of the Interior, 1950.

Gill, Frank. *Ornithology,* 2nd ed. New York: W.H. Freeman & Company, 1995.

Godfrey, W. Earl. *The Birds of Canada*, rev. ed. Ottawa: National Museum of Natural Sciences, 1986.

Harrison, Hal H. *Birds' Nests*. Boston: Houghton Mifflin Company, 1975.

Jones, John Oliver. *Where the Birds Are*. New York: Morrow, 1990.

_____. *The US Outdoor Atlas & Recreation Guide*. Boston: Houghton Mifflin Company, 1992.

Kaufman, Kenn. *Field Guide to North American Birds*. Boston: Houghton Mifflin, 2000.

Lofgren, Lars. *Ocean Birds*. Toronto: Johnston & Company, 1984.

Marzluff, John M., and Rex Sallabanks. *Avian Conservation*. Washington: Island Press, 1998.

McElroy, Jr., Thomas P. *The Habitat Guide to Birding: A Guide to Birding East of the Rockies*. New York: Knopf, 1974.

Mountford, Guy. *Rare Birds of the World*. London: Collins, 1988.

National Wildlife Federation and American Bird Conservancy. *The Birdwatcher's Guide to Global Warming*. Washington: National Wildlife Federation & American Bird Conservancy, 2002.

NatureServe. 2007. *NatureServe Explorer: An Online Encyclopedia of Life [web application]*. Version 5.0. Arlington: NatureServe. Available at www.natureserve.org/explorer.

Peterson, Roger Tory. *Eastern Birds*. Boston: Houghton Mifflin, 1980.

Poole, A., and F. Gill, eds. *The Birds of North America: Life Histories for the 21st Century*. Washington: The Birds of North America Inc., 1992.

Pough, Richard H. *Audubon Guides, All the Birds of Eastern and Central North America.* Garden City, NY: Doubleday, 1953.

Prager, Ellen J., and Sylvia Earle. *The Oceans.* New York: McGraw-Hill, 2000.

Ridgely, R.S., et al. *Digital Distribution Maps of the Birds of the Western Hemisphere, version 1.0.*Arlington: NatureServe, 2003.

Robbins, Chandler S., Bertel Bruun, Herbert S. Zim, and Arthur Singer. *Birds of North America*, exp. and rev. ed. New York: Golden, 1983.

Schreiber, E.A., and Joanna Burger, eds. *Biology of Marine Birds.* Boca Raton, FL: CRC Press, 2002.

Sibley, David Allen. *The Sibley Guide to Birds.* New York: Knopf, 2000.

Sibley, David Allen, John B. Dunning, Jr., and Chris Elphick, eds. *The Sibley Guide to Bird Life & Behavior.* New York: Knopf, 2001.

Skutch, Alexander F. *Origins of Nature's Beauty.* Austin: The University of Texas Press, 1992.

_____. *The Minds of Birds.* College Station, TX: Texas A&M University Press, 1996.

Stokes, Donald, and Lillian Stokes. *A Guide to Bird Behavior*, vols. 1, 2, 3. Boston: Little, Brown, 1979, 1983, 1989.

Teale, Edwin Way. *Green Treasury.* New York: Dodd, Mead & Company, 1952.

Tudge, Colin. *The Variety of Life.* New York: Oxford University Press, 2000.

Tufts, Robie W. *Birds of Nova Scotia*, 3rd ed. Halifax: Nimbus Publishing/Nova Scotia Museum, 1986.

Wernert, Susan, ed. *North American Wildlife.* Pleasantville, NY: Reader's Digest Association, 1982.

SELECTED SEABIRD AND COASTAL BIRD AREAS IN CANADA

FUNK ISLAND ECOLOGICAL RESERVE
Parks & Natural Areas Division
Dept. of Environment and Conservation
Government of Newfoundland and Labrador
33 Reid's Lane
Deer Lake, NL A8A 2A3
709-635-4520
www.env.gov.nl.ca/parks/wer

Although the general public is not permitted to visit, Funk Island must be included in this list since it is one of the most important seabird nesting islands in North America. Despite its minute size of some 500 acres, this tiny island, located 40 miles off the east coast of Newfoundland, is home to over a million seabirds. It is the largest common murre breeding colony in the western Atlantic, and several other species, such as thick-billed murre, northern gannet, northern fulmar, Atlantic puffin and razorbill also nest there. In historic times, Funk Island was the location of one of the largest breeding colonies of the extinct great auk.

BACCALIEU ISLAND ECOLOGICAL RESERVE
Parks & Natural Areas Division
Dept. of Environment and Conservation
Government of Newfoundland and Labrador
33 Reid's Lane
Deer Lake, NL A8A 2A3
709-635-4520
www.env.gov.nl.ca/parks/wer

Possibly the largest seabird breeding colony anywhere in the world,

Baccalieu Island's 1,200 acres is host to some 7 million seabirds, including the world's largest colony of Leach's storm-petrel. Other species include northern gannet, Atlantic puffin, common and thick-billed murre and northern fulmar. The island is somewhat difficult to visit, but can be viewed from the mainland of Newfoundland from Bay de Verde at the northeastern tip of the Avalon Peninsula. A permit is required to land by boat at the nesting areas, and although currently no licensed boat operators do tours to the island, it's worth contacting the above office to see if this situation has changed.

CAPE ST. MARY'S ECOLOGICAL RESERVE
Parks & Natural Areas Division
Dept. of Environment and Conservation
Government of Newfoundland and Labrador
33 Reid's Lane
Deer Lake, NL A8A 2A3
709-635-4520
www.env.gov.nl.ca/parks/wer

Cape St. Mary's is one of the most accessible and spectacular seabird colonies anywhere in the world. Located about two hours southwest of St. John's. A half-mile trail from the parking lot brings you to the edge of a raucous colony of nesting birds that includes 24,000 northern gannets, 20,000 black-legged kittiwakes, 20,000 common murres, and a variety of other breeding seabirds. Much of the gannet colony is located atop a 300-foot-high sea stack that sits only some 50 feet from a viewing area at the edge of the cliff. A new, large interpretation centre has recently been built beside the parking lot.

WITLESS BAY ECOLOGICAL RESERVE
Parks & Natural Areas Division
Dept. of Environment and Conservation
Government of Newfoundland and Labrador
33 Reid's Lane
Deer Lake, NL A8A 2A3
709-635-4520
www.env.gov.nl.ca/parks/wer

Located a half-hour south of St. John's, this reserve is made up of Green, Great, Gull and Pee-Pee Islands. Though the entire reserve is 12 square miles in extent, most of that is ocean, with less than 1 square mile comprised of islands. North America's largest colony of Atlantic puffins, with more than 500,000 birds, is located here, as is the world's second-largest Leach's storm-petrel colony with over 1 million birds. Although landing on the islands is generally prohibited, the birds can be seen up close by taking one of the several commercial boat tours that operate during the seabird breeding season.

BIRD ISLANDS (HERTFORD AND CIBOUX ISLANDS)
Sanctuaries and Wildlife Management Areas
Wildlife Division
Nova Scotia Department of Natural Resources
136 Exhibition St.
Kentville, N.S. B4N 4E5
902-679-6176
www.gov.ns.ca/natr/wildlife/sanctuaries/

These two small islands are home to Nova Scotia's largest seabird colony. Located off the coast of Cape Breton Island, an hour from Sydney, the islands are home to breeding Atlantic puffins, razorbills, black-legged kittiwakes, black guillemots and the largest colony of great cormorants in North America. Commercial birding boat tours to the islands are available.

BRIER ISLAND, NOVA SCOTIA
www.brierisland.org
info@brierisland.org

This 4-mile-long by 1.5-mile-wide island in the lower Bay of Fundy is a hotspot for seabirds. The shorelines and beaches are teeming with shorebirds during the fall migration season and the highly mixed, tidal waters surrounding the island attract large numbers of seabirds and coastal birds such as shearwaters, northern gannets, Atlantic puffins, phalaropes, jaegers, common eiders, skuas and terns. Several commercial operators run boat tours to observe seabirds as well as the abundant whales around the island.

MACHIAS SEAL ISLAND, BAY OF FUNDY
Canadian Wildlife Service
P.O. Box 6227
Sackville, New Brunswick E4L 1G6
506-364-5044
www.cws-scf.ec.gc.ca

This small 15-acre island, located between the Maine coast and Grand Manan Island, is one of the most important seabird nesting sites in the Bay of Fundy. One of the most southerly North American colonies of Atlantic puffins (approximately 1,000 pairs) is located here. Razorbills, Arctic and common terns and common eiders also breed. Although several commercial boat tours to the island are available (from both the State of Maine and from Grand Manan Island in New Brunswick), access to the islands is strictly controlled and visits must be done with licensed guides.

GRAND MANAN ISLAND AREA, NEW BRUNSWICK
Grand Manan Tourism
1141 Rte. 776, Grand Manan, N.B. E5G 4E9
888-525-1655
www.grandmanannb.com

The largest island in the Bay of Fundy is located in an area rich in marine birds and marine mammals. Common murres, northern gannets, black-legged kittiwakes, shearwaters, razorbills, Atlantic puffins, several sea duck species, phalaropes and jaegers can be seen at sea at the appropriate times of year. The waters around the main island and the smaller islands are rich in the food seabirds like to eat. The 90-minute ferry ride from the mainland also provides excellent opportunities to observe seabirds. Tours to Machias Seal Island, just a few miles away, embark from Grand Manan.

BONAVENTURE ISLAND AND PERCE ROCK MIGRATORY
BIRD SANCTUARY
Canadian Wildlife Service
1141, route de l'Eglise
C.P. 10100, 9e étage

Sainte-Foy, QC G1V 4H5
418-782-2240
www.qc.ec.gc.ca/faune/faune/html/mbs_ile_bonaventure.html

One of the most important seabird nesting colonies in the Gulf of St. Lawrence. With over 30,000 nesting pairs, this nearly 1,200-acre island supports the largest colony of northern gannets in North America. Also found here are about 12,000 breeding pairs of black-legged kittiwake and 14,000 pairs of common murre. Other breeding species include the herring and great black-backed gulls, Atlantic puffin, razorbill, black guillemot and Leach's storm-petrel. Great and double-crested cormorants nest on Percé Rock. Commercial boat tours to the island are available during the breeding season.

SCOTT ISLANDS ARCHIPELAGO, VANCOUVER ISLAND, BC
Canadian Parks and Wilderness Society
610-555 West Georgia St.
Vancouver, BC V6B 1Z6
604-685-7445
www.cpawsbc.org

This archipelago of small islands, located off the northern tip of Vancouver Island, is one of the most biologically rich marine ecosystems on Canada's Pacific coast. Over 2 million nesting seabirds, or nearly half of the breeding population in British Columbia, are found here. Tufted puffins, common murres, pigeon guillemots, Cassin's and rhinoceros auklets and several other species nest here. The waters around the islands are an important north Pacific feeding area for the black-footed albatross, which is found in considerable numbers here.

ESQUIMALT LAGOON MIGRATORY BIRD SANCTUARY,
VANCOUVER ISLAND
Canadian Wildlife Service
Pacific Wildlife Research Centre
RR#1, 5421 Robertson Rd.
Delta, BC V4K 3N2
604-940-4700
www.esquimaltlagoon.com

This federal migratory bird sanctuary is located near the city of Victoria. Its 317 acres are comprised largely of a saltwater tidal lagoon on the Strait of Georgia. An excellent site to observe a variety of gulls, including Heerman's, Bonaparte's, California, mew, glaucous-winged and ring-billed. Shorebirds include black oyster-catchers, dunlins, black-bellied plovers and sanderlings. Outside the lagoon, in the Strait of Georgia, several species of cormorant can be seen, as well as murres, white-winged and surf scoters, Barrow's goldeneye, long-tailed duck and brant.

GWAII HAANAS NATIONAL PARK RESERVE,
QUEEN CHARLOTTE ISLANDS
Parks Canada
60 Second Beach Rd.
Skidegate, P.O. Box 37
Queen Charlotte, B.C. V0T 1S0
250-559-8818
www.pc.gc.ca/pn-np/bc/gwaiihaanas/index_e.asp

Comprising nearly 600 square miles and 138 islands, this immensely beautiful and wild national park reserve hosts an estimated 1.5 million seabirds that nest along its 2,900 miles of shoreline. Species breeding here include both horned and tufted puffins, Leach's storm-petrel, common murre, rhinoceros and Cassin's auklets, pigeon guillemot, ancient murrelet and pelagic cormorant.

SELECTED SEABIRD AND COASTAL BIRD AREAS IN THE UNITED STATES

ALASKA MARITIME NATIONAL WILDLIFE REFUGE
Aleutian Islands Unit
95 Sterling Highway, Suite 1 MS505
Homer, AK 99603
907-235-6546
http://alaskamaritime.fws.gov

Although this refuge is quite inaccessible to the public it is included here because it is part of the largest marine reserve in North America and is home to over 10 million seabirds. This 1.3 million acre chain of some 200 volcanic islands stretches for 1,100 miles from Alaska west into the Bering Sea. The Aleutians provide refuge for puffins, murres, auks, auklets, fulmars, kittiwakes, terns, gulls, sea ducks and shorebirds. Non-breeding, pelagic species such as shearwaters and albatrosses are also found here. One of the most important marine areas on the planet.

TOGIAK NATIONAL WILDLIFE REFUGE
P.O. Box 270 MS569
Dillingham, AK 99627-0069
907-842-1063
http://togiak.fws.gov

Another large refuge at over 4 million acres, Togiak is located in southwestern Alaska. It is a vital area for breeding seabirds and millions of murres, gulls, auks, horned puffins, gulls and cormorants nest on its coastal headlands. Cape Pierce and Cape Newenham are particularly large seabird colonies. Large numbers of waterfowl also inhabit the reserve and it is an important migration site for shorebirds.

KENAI FJORDS NATIONAL PARK
P.O. Box 1727
Seward, AK 99664
907-224-7500
www.nps.gov/kefj/

This 670,000-acre park, located south of Anchorage, encompasses rich rain forests and fjords. The park's north Pacific coastline, islands and marine waters are habitat to tens of thousands of breeding seabirds, including two species of puffin, black-legged kittiwakes, common murres and a variety of gull species.

SANTA CRUZ ISLAND RESERVE
The Nature Conservancy
201 Mission St., 4th Floor
San Francisco, CA 94105-1832
415-777-0487
www.nature.org

This 62,000-acre island, located some 20 miles off the coast of Santa Barbara, is owned by the Nature Conservancy and the National Parks Service. The island boasts a diversity of birds including large numbers of seabirds. Access is by boat only.

FARALLON NATIONAL WILDLIFE REFUGE
c/o Don Edwards San Francisco Bay National Wildlife Refuge Complex
P.O. Box 524
Newark, CA. 94560-0524
www.fws.gov/sfbayrefuges/farallon/farallon.htm

Located 30 miles west of San Francisco, the small 211-acre Farallon Islands comprise the largest seabird colony in California with some 300,000 breeding birds. Leach's storm-petrels, western gulls, brown pelicans, Cassin's and rhinoceros auklets, common murres and black oystercatchers all nest here. Several pelagic species may be observed, including the black-footed albatross and the Buller's shearwater. Although the islands are closed to the public, wildlife can be viewed from boats. One-day boat trips for the public are offered between June and November.

HUMBOLDT BAY NATIONAL WILDLIFE REFUGE
P.O. 576
1020 Ranch Road
Loleta, CA 95551-9633
www.fws.gov/humboldtbay/

This northern California refuge is located near Eureka. The refuge's 2,000-plus acres are comprised largely of estuaries and coastal habitat. Fourteen-acre Castle Rock Island, part of the refuge, is located just a mile offshore. Despite its small size, this refuge is the second-largest seabird nesting colony in California and boasts the largest breeding population of common murres in the state.

DUNGENESS NATIONAL WILDLIFE REFUGE
Sequim, WA.
360-457-8451
http://pacific.fws.gov/refuges/field/wa_dungeness.htm

An enormous sand spit jutting for over 5 miles into the Strait of Juan de Fuca. This refuge covers over 700 acres and is an important area for nesting, migrating and wintering shorebirds and waterfowl such as turnstones, phalaropes, dunlins, brant, white-winged and surf scoters and harlequin ducks, among others.

GULF ISLANDS NATIONAL SEASHORE
1801 Gulf Breeze Parkway
Gulf Breeze, FL 32563
850-934-2600
www.nps.gov/guis/index.htm

This large national seashore, over 60,000 acres in area, is located in both Florida and Mississippi. A complex of beaches, sandbars and low-lying coast, it is habitat for a variety of waterfowl as well as wintering and migrating shorebirds. Magnificent frigatebirds and two species of booby may be seen in the summer.

DELTA NATIONAL WILDLIFE REFUGE AND BRETON ISLANDS
NATIONAL WILDLIFE REFUGE
Venice, LA 70091
985-534-2269
www.fws.gov/delta/

Located in the middle of the Mississippi delta, this refuge contains about 50,000 acres of bayous, salt marshes and ponds. The Breton Islands portion is made up of sandy beach habitat and salt marshes. Several species of terns nest here including royal, Sandwich and Caspian terns, as well as laughing gulls and black skimmers. The brown pelican also nests. Dunlin, ruddy turnstone, whimbrel and other shorebirds are common in winter or during migration. Magnificent frigatebirds are a possibility. Refuge is accessible only by boat.

MAINE COASTAL ISLANDS NATIONAL WILDLIFE REFUGE
P.O. Box 279
Milbridge, ME 04658
207-546-2124
www.fws.gov/northeast/mainecoastal/

A complex of 47 offshore islands and coastal sections, this important refuge totals over 7,400 acres along Maine's north coast. The most important seabird nesting area left in the northeastern U.S., the refuge contains colonies of Atlantic puffin, razorbill, black guillemot and Leach's storm-petrel. Colonies of Arctic tern and the endangered roseate tern are located within the refuge. The islands are generally closed to the public. The coastal sections offer opportunities for birders.

MONOMOY ISLAND NATIONAL WILDLIFE REFUGE
Wikis Way, Morris Island
Chatham, MA. 02633
508-945-0594
www.fws.gov/northeast/monomoy

Over 2,000 acres of dunes, salt marshes, freshwater marshes and freshwater ponds located at the elbow of Cape Cod on Monomoy and Morris Islands. An extremely important shorebird migration site, as well as important wintering habitat for sea ducks, including scoters, common eiders, brants, red-breasted mergansers, long-tail ducks and buffleheads. Laughing gulls, roseate and least terns breed on the islands.

EDWIN B. FORSYTHE NATIONAL WILDLIFE REFUGE
Box 72
Oceanville, NJ 08231
609-652-1665
www.fws.gov/northeast/forsythe/

The refuge is made up of 34,000 acres of coastal salt meadows, salt marshes, low-lying coast, beaches and open bays. The area is an important shorebird migration site for species such as ruddy turnstone, sanderling and dunlin. Brant, great black-backed gull, black skimmer and a variety of other species also rely on the refuge.

The Barnegat light is an important breeding area for common terns, as well as being good for observing sea ducks during the winter.

SEABIRD AND COASTAL BIRD INTERNET RESOURCES

Below are names and website addresses for a selection of groups that are involved in bird conservation and birding in North America. All of these organizations carry out important conservation work and they need our support. Some of the websites, especially those of NatureServe, BirdSource and the Cornell Laboratory of Ornithology, are great learning resources, offering an astonishing amount of information about the natural history and conservation of birds.

AMERICAN BIRD CONSERVANCY
www.abcbirds.org

AMERICAN BIRDING
ASSOCIATION
www.americanbirding.org

BIRDLIFE INTERNATIONAL
GLOBAL SEABIRD PROGRAMME
www.birdlife.net

BIRDSOURCE
www.birdsource.org

BIRD STUDIES CANADA
www.bsc-eoc.org

CANADIAN NATURE FEDERATION
www.cnf.ca/bird

CORNELL LABORATORY
OF ORNITHOLOGY
www.birds.cornell.edu

NATIONAL AUDUBON SOCIETY
www.audubon.org

NATURESERVE
www.natureserve.org

NEW ENGLAND SEABIRDS
www.neseabirds.com

NORTH AMERICAN BIRD
CONSERVATION INITIATIVE
www.nabci.net

OCEAN WANDERERS
www.oceanwanderers.com

PARTNERS IN FLIGHT
www.partnersinflight.org

SAVE THE ALBATROSS
www.savethealbatross.net

WORLD WILDLIFE FUND
OF CANADA
www.wwf.ca

ACKNOWLEDGMENTS

Thank you to Paula Leslie for her assistance in the field.

Thanks to Jack and Jean Leslie for their continued support and enthusiasm, and to Bev and Jacob.

Thanks to NatureServe for once again granting permission to use its Western Hemisphere range maps and distribution maps.

Thanks to Michael Mouland, Marijke Friesen and the staff of Key Porter Books.

PHOTO CREDITS

All photos in the book by Scott Leslie except the following:

pages 51, 58, 144, 147, 213, 216, Peter LaTourette
page 127, Steve Byland/123RF
pages 129, 132, 201, Steffen Foerster/123RF
page 130, nialat/123RF
page 54 David Woods/123RF
page 78, Mark Van Overmeire/123RF
page 80, David Brimm/123RF
page 154, D. Otte/123RF
page 156, Dimitry Mavlov/123RF
page 169, David Levinson/123RF
page 171, Harris Shiffman
page 218, Steve Estavanik/123RF

INDEX